Angela Small

CHRISTMAS STORIES
FROM AROUND THE WORLD:
HONORING JESUS IN MANY LANDS

Also by J. Lawrence Driskill

Cross-Cultural Marriages and the Church

Japan Diary of Cross-Cultural Mission

Mission Adventures in Many Lands

Mission Stories from Around the World

Worldwide Mission Stories for Young People

CHRISTMAS STORIES
FROM AROUND THE WORLD:
HONORING JESUS IN MANY LANDS

●

J. LAWRENCE DRISKILL, EDITOR

Hope Publishing House
Pasadena, California

Copyright © 1997 J. Lawrence Driskill

For information address:
Hope Publishing House
Southern California Ecumenical Council
P.O. Box 60008
Pasadena, CA 91116 - U.S.A.
Tel: (818) 792-6123 / Fax: (818) 792-2121

Cover design — Michael McClary/The Workshop

Printed in the U.S.A. on acid-free paper

Library of Congress Cataloging-in-Publication Data

Christmas stories from around the world : honoring Jesus in many lands
/ J. Lawrence Driskill, editor.
    p.   cm.
    ISBN 0-932727-87-5 trade paper.) -- ISBN 0-932727-88-3 lib. hc)
    1. Christmas--Cross-cultural studies.   I. Driskill, J. Lawrence,
1920-
GT4985.C543 1997
394.2'663--dc20   96-38177
                                                CIP

Gratefully dedicated

to those who shared

their Christmas experiences

from around the world.

His Gift

by James B. Douthitt

The finest present we can bring
At Christmas to our Lord and King
Is not in tributes — cold and chill
And talking of world-wide good will;
Is not in gifts on lovely tree
Nor e'en in music glad and free.

The finest present we can bring
At Christmas to our Lord and King
Is hearts' devotion, full and true
Filled with his blessed love anew.
Yes, give him garlands, song and gold
But give your self — the gift untold.

Acknowledgements

First I want to thank those who kindly shared their Christmas experiences from around the world. Their stories are the basic foundation for this book.

I also need to thank Ms. Osanna Love Gooding and the Westminster Gardens Writers' Group for their comments and suggestions. Ms. Gooding also wrote the foreword.

Four Christian leaders provided helpful commendations: Dr. Clifton Kirkpatrick, Dr. Gordon Kirk, Dr. Les Blank and Rev. Tom Wentz.

Mrs. Betty Kiriyama prepared the computer disk, and my editor and publisher Faith Annette Sand did the vital work of editing and publishing.

Most of all, I thank God who came to us in Jesus Christ, providing the basis for Christmas love and joy.

Contents

PART I — Christmas Stories from Around the World

PART II — Christmas Traditions Around the World

Foreword

Dr. J. Lawrence Driskill, former missionary to Japan, has edited this delightful Christmas book for all ages. Most of these true Christmas tales are written by missionaries from many countries in the world. Here they share some of their Yuletide experiences with Christ's followers on every continent.

Christmas celebrations in their multi-cultural diversity are of interest to all who are curious about spiritual beliefs and customs as they are practiced around our globe. What especially amazes us in the West is to realize the depth of love and gratitude these so-called materially deprived Christians feel for their loving and forgiving Savior.

How does an "Untouchable" doctor, educated by missionaries to India, worship the Christ Child? How is a young African boy able to give up a beloved Christmas present in order to go beyond "looking good" to enter more deeply into his prayer life with Jesus? And what Christmas present does a penniless, rehabilitated teenaged prostitute in Korea give to the Baby Jesus as she kneels before the Manger during a Christmas pageant?

The second part of this book answers those questions you never stopped to research about the origins, meaning, music, pageants, literature, customs and traditions of Christmas. Dr. Driskill has produced a valuable reference book for the whole family.
— *(Osanna) Phyllis Love Gooding, Director*
Westminster Gardens Writers' Group

Introduction

The Christmas carol "Joy to the world! the Lord is come" emphasizes that Christmas love and joy are God's gift to the whole world. Christmas is celebrated today by billions of people in almost every country. Jesus Christ is a world Savior. Although every country has its own way of celebrating Christmas, the theme of God's love and salvation through Jesus Christ binds all Christmas celebrations together. Thankfully the joy of salvation rings out to every nation, race and people's group.

Christians know that Jesus Christ is the "reason for the season." The stories in this book reveal how Christians celebrate Christ's love and saving power in many lands — sometimes under difficult circumstances. Darkness threatens every country but Christ can bring light and hope to every corner of the world. Some denounce secular celebrations of Christmas. To them songs like "White Christmas" and "Jingle Bells" sound shallow and empty. I can understand such criticism, but after many years as a missionary in a non-Christian culture, it seems to me that department store Christmas decorations and secular Christmas songs can serve to whet the interest for later planting the gospel seed and reaping the harvest of salvation. Surrounded by Christmas celebrations, one will eventually ask, "What is behind this?" Therefore this book discusses both religious and secular celebrations of Christmas.

Please join in praying that this book will help glorify the Christ of Christmas. "Be not afraid ... for to you is born ... a Savior, who is Christ the Lord" (Lk 2:1-11).

— Dr. J. Lawrence Driskill, editor

No Room

by James B. Douthitt

(see Luke 2:7)

No room for Christ in
  Bethlehem
When Joseph sought a
  place
For men were filled with
  other cares
And would not give him
  space.

No room for Christ in
  Nazareth
Because he dared to give
The story of God's blessed
  plan
That all mankind should
  live.

No room for Christ in
  synagogue
For greed had banished
  love
Men cherished men's com-
  mandments more
Than God's Word from
  above.

No room for Christ in
  Roman world
Where military might
Subjected all to strength of
  sword
To power instead of right.

Just room for Christ on
  Calvary
Where thieves were cruci-
  fied
Because he came to teach
  men love
Our Lord and Savior died.

No room for Christ in
  modern world
Where mammon holds full
  sway
Where greed and hatred,
  lust and sin
Crowd out his blessed
  way.

O Christian, do you give
  him room
In motive, word, and deed?
Do you thrust out conflict-
  ing thoughts
And his commandments
  heed?

If only men would give
  him room
Soon sin and war would
  cease
And all the world unite to
  serve
The blessed Prince of
  Peace!

Part I

Christmas Stories from Around the World

1

Beatrice and Ted Stevenson

A Hot and Muggy Christmas in India

by **Beatrice Stevenson**

It was hot and muggy that Christmas. The town with its drab mud walls and the heavy odor of dung that hung in the air seemed just plain dirty. I was unhappy that my husband had agreed to come as a visiting surgeon to the Miraj Medical Center in West India. In the midst of the heat, far from our home and our children, I found it difficult to celebrate or feel any joy that season — until Christmas Eve when we attended a most unusual Christmas pageant.

At first I had found India quite fascinating — the temple festivals, the elephants and the cheetahs in the local maharajah's stable, the women in their colorful saris gracefully balancing water jars on their heads, the narrow village streets chaotically crowded with logjams of people, goats, bullock-carts, bikes and honking buses.

Suddenly my world changed — I became a patient in the hospital myself. In my pain and weakness I felt all the glamour evaporate. "How," I thought miserably, "can I ever celebrate Christmas in this alien place?"

As the sun went down Christmas Eve, carpenters and electricians were still putting final touches on a large outdoor stage. Already the courtyard was packed with curious townsfolk sitting cross-legged on the ground, their buzz of talk rising in an increasing crescendo like a hive of swarming bees. In the foreground squatted hundreds of noisy, restless kids.

Backstage the cast was in near panic: "I can't make these wings stay on!" "Where's the third Magi's crown?" "Somebody, please help me with this halo!" Mary was afraid of her donkey ("I've never ridden one before!"). It seemed improbable these amateurs could pull off a credible performance in this bedlam.

Suddenly the miracle began. As the stage lights flashed on, an expectant hush fell on the waiting crowd. From the street came the clatter of hooves. A shaggy donkey tagged along by its little foal appeared out of the night, a drooping Mary on its back. Joseph followed, busily thwacking a branch on the donkey's rump and uttering salty admonitions to keep the pair moving. On stage a voluble and frantic innkeeper drove them away from his inn. Nearby some ragged goatherds warmed their hands at a small fire, while real goats and their kids milled, bleating, among them.

Then a burst of music filtered into the night as a throng of angels — with waist-long black hair blowing in the night breeze — began singing Marathi Christmas carols from raised platforms above the stage and from the second-floor balconies surrounding it. Spotlights picked out a rustic grotto, where a real baby (borrowed from the obstetrics ward) lay in a straw-filled trough. The Magi entered, resplendent in satin robes of crimson, gold and royal purple (the third one appeared in a turban, his crown apparently still lost). Surrounded by goat-herds, they knelt to offer their precious gifts to the baby, while Mary, her blue sari framing a sweet young face, bent over the baby in wondering devotion.

As I watched the rapt audience, I knew the women there could identify with this young mother who had given birth to her babe in the squalor of a cattle shed. For centuries Indian women have birthed their babies in dark, mud-floored back-rooms, attended only by a midwife and then separated for ten days of purification, shut off from husband and family.

What a difference in this Christmas story — Mary's husband stood close by, caring and protective. It was a lovely and moving tableau. So realistic, it almost seemed the little Lord Jesus had been born anew. Never had Christmas pageants back home affected me so with their plastic doll babies, Magi dressed in striped bathrobes and angels either waving to the audience or giggling uncontrollably.

More was to come. Suddenly anguished cries from the angels electrified the audience as an enormous shadow of a cross was flung up on the wall above the manger scene.

"What is this?" an angel cried in horror. "Is this to be the fate of our innocent baby?"

"Who would do this dreadful thing to the little Lord of

Heaven?" another angel wailed, wringing her hands.

A chorus of angels cried out, "Who will help him?"

I watched in suspense as a band of soldiers, with guns and truncheons, marched across the stage. Their leader, pausing at the manger, said contemptuously: "What can a helpless babe do? The only power in this world comes from the mouth of a gun!" Off he marched with his men.

A ragged beggar hobbled up, leaning on a crutch, his feet bandaged, a begging bowl in his hand. "Little one," he said to the baby, "What good am I to you? I am only a beggar, faint with hunger and wretched with pain. I cannot help you. Neither can you help me for this sad life is my fate — my karma." He stumbled off, moaning softly to himself.

Next across the stage came a gaunt young mother with a baby on her hip, two small children clinging to her sari. "I'm so harassed by these children I can't think of anything else," she explained to Mary. "Maybe later — when they're older — I can come back ..." Her voice trailed off as she moved wearily on with her brood.

A bearded guru appeared, a pile of sacred books under his arm. "I worship many gods," he said haughtily to the babe. "If you want to be one of them, you may. I don't mind. I'm very broad-minded. But to follow you only — how ridiculous! I need gods for every occasion; one simply will not do." With an arrogant toss of his head he strode away.

At this point the angels who had covered their eyes with shame at this sacrilege, cried out to the audience: "Is there no one here who will give allegiance to the King of Heaven? God's very Son has come to help us. Does this mean nothing to you?"

The audience stirred uneasily, troubled by this appeal.

Suddenly there was a fresh craning of necks as a smiling

young woman, in white sari and nurse's cap, mounted the stage and knelt before the manger. "Gladly will I serve you, O Lord, my King," she exclaimed, "because you have made all the difference in my life!"

Turning to the startled crowd she said: "I come from the southernmost state of Kerala and there we have followed the Christ for almost 2,000 years, ever since his disciple Saint Thomas came to India to tell us the Good News." Pointing to the shadowed cross above the manger, she continued, "God's own Son died on a cross like that to pay for our sins so that we could become sons and daughters of Almighty God.

"For me this has meant growing up in a loving Christian family where I was just as important as my brothers, where I too had schooling and where, instead of being married off at puberty, I was allowed to choose my own career and husband. I have a happy home here and serve the Lord I love by nursing in this hospital."

A worker with a garden hoe in hand came forward and joined her. Also kneeling by the manger, he cried out: "O Lord my Savior, I owe you everything — my life, my health, my new standing in this Christian community. Gladly will I serve you all the days of my life!"

He explained to the audience, "I once had leprosy. I was an outcast, doomed to a life of begging until I heard about this Christian hospital. Here doctors cured my leprosy and operated on my useless claw-like hands. Look!" he exclaimed, holding his hoe aloft, "Now my fingers can bend and hold things again. I'm a gardener here and tend the hospital's garden. At last I'm useful and have worth. I praise the Lord for this."

Finally a dignified older man in surgeon's cap and gown approached the manger, prostrated himself before its baby and turned to the audience to say: "You know me well, my friends. I am Dr. Chopade, a surgeon here at Miraj Medical Center. I've cared for many of you over the past 20 years. But what you may not know is that I was an 'untouchable.'"

A startled murmur swept through the crowd, but his kind voice continued: "Yes, according to your law I was 'unholy' — a non-person — not created by the gods as you are. As a boy I lived in a segregated part of our village. My widowed mother cleaned latrines for a living and I rummaged through the village garbage, competing with dogs for something to satisfy our hunger. Such 'dirty work' was all we were permitted to do. The common well, the bazaar shops, the village school were all out-of-bounds for me."

"That's right!" "They should be!" angry voices shouted from the courtyard. "You have no place in them!"

Dr. Chopade seemed not to hear and continued quietly: "But I wanted to be someone. Especially I wanted to be a doctor like the ones I had seen from the mission hospital who tended the sick in our village, so I would sit as close to the school as I dared and listen to the teacher's lessons. He often cursed me. The children would chase me away with stones," the surgeon confessed as approving catcalls came from the audience, "but each day I'd be back."

"Then I learned something wonderful. There were missionaries from across the sea who actually wanted to help 'untouchables.' Their school was many kilometers away, but somehow I found my way there — and these foreigners welcomed me. They even gave me a work scholarship — me, an 'untouchable'! Eventually, with their help, I graduated from college and medical school — and here I am, praising my Lord and serving my people in his name."

For a long moment he gazed out over the crowd, his dark eyes tender and pleading. Then, turning back to the manger, he pressed his palms together in the classic Indian greeting and murmured: "Thank you! Thank you, Lord Jesus!"

From the angels above the stage and the surrounding balconies floated a final song:

> Silent night, holy night!
> Son of God, love's pure light ...
> With the angels let us sing,
> Alleluia to our King;
> Christ the Savior is born.

For a moment the audience sat transfixed. Then, in complete silence, they rose and moved away to their dark streets and homes.

A night breeze rustled the palm trees. Overhead a full moon rode the clouds in splendor. I was moved to tears by this real-life Christmas drama.

Suddenly there was a burst of firecrackers and bright explosions of light overhead — and I found myself laughing.

Of course! How right and appropriate was this exuberant, staccato rejoicing — the traditional way in Eastern lands to celebrate the birthday of a King! Although I was still a long way from home, that lovely Christmas pageant brought the season's joy back to my soul and I was glad for this rare opportunity to participate in a holiday celebration like none I'd ever had before.

2

Gayle Beanland

The Cameroon Christmas Box

by Gayle Beanland

"Angondo!" (Cool!) said Albert in his national language of
Bulu, "It's *great* to be back in the bush!" In his hand was a bow
and on his back was a quiver of homemade arrows. His brother
Ndi preceded him with a machete, hacking their way through
the high savanna grass toward a grove of trees where they knew
lived a band of monkeys.

Atangana, their father, had helped them make the bows and
arrows. He and other villagers had long before taught them the
rudimentary lessons of hunting but the lads could not hunt
often. Now they lived in the city where the urban conditions
were far different from the surroundings of their family village.

This was a rare day for them to be in the forest and they were enjoying every moment of it. Early they had left home, riding one of the noisy mammy-wagons that at all hours rolled out of the city. Albert and Ndi had come with Atangana and their mother, Njama for the day.

Before long, the boys returned to the village accompanied by their barkless basenji hunting dogs whose neck-bells announced their presence. On a pole between them dangled a monkey that had been unable to escape Albert's marksmanship; on another shaft, lugged on the shoulders of two of their friends, was a young deer shot by Ndi.

The mood of the village changed dramatically with their entrance. Preparation for dinner was halted long enough to include the results of the chase in which Albert and Ndi had played a prominent part.

After a delicious dinner of their meat accompanied by peanut soup and generous portions of the foul-smelling but delicious *kank*-bread called *bibobola,* their fulfilling day ended and they were ready to return to Yaounde where Atangana worked for my parents.

Atangana was a superb cook, well-trained in culinary arts by my mother, a Southerner who possessed unparalleled skills in the kitchen. Often Atangana's inventory of wild game was provided by my father's "shoot-man," Ze Tonga, who daily went into the nearby forest with Dad's double-barreled shotgun. Seldom did he return without something on his shoulder evidencing a successful shoot. Results of this forest venture were shared with all the others living in the mission complex.

Assisting the household were Frida Bita, the nanny of my unmanageable brother, and M'voe who looked after me. Their presence enabled our mother to be at school the better part of

9

her day helping equip the teachers in their pedagogical tasks.

Our home on the brow of a hill was a whitewashed adobe-brick house surrounded by a wide porch from which you could see across the wide plain the seven hills of Yaounde — much like the seven hills of Rome. It was on this porch that my brother and I along with Albert and Ndi played endlessly. Atangana and his family lived next door as did Ze Tonga and his family as well as Frida and M'voe.

We were all part of an extended family, working together, for in the Bulu ethic to work for a family is to become an integral part of that household. The Christmas holidays were a time of joyful exchanging gifts as we celebrated God's Christmas gift of his son to the world by giving one another gifts — usually animals such as goats or chickens, or sometimes eggs, bolts of cloth, jewelry or some type of clothing.

Christmas also brought special packages from America. When such a box arrived, my father would put it on the dining room table where we would crowd around waiting excitedly. When all had gathered, he would cut the strings, rip open the paper, as we strained to see what was in the box.

How magnificent to smell the lovely aromas emanating from the United States. The dank humidity of Africa impregnates everything with an omnipresent smell of mildew, so the breathtaking fragrances encapsulated in those packages were a special treat.

I'll never forget a particular box that came from an aunt in Mississippi when I was eight for it contained a pair of lovely blue shorts that fit me perfectly. The color blue is a favorite for many Africans and this was an especially brilliant blue that attracted a lot of attention from my friends. Being special, I only wore them on Sunday for church. Each Sunday, Ndi would walk up, ogle them, then run his hands along the cloth, uttering sounds of elation.

Having seen this happen several weeks in a row, Mother sent a hurried letter off to the States asking my aunt either to get another pair of similar trousers or send her some cloth with which to make them, since nothing similar was available in Cameroon. It took awhile, but finally some six months later a package arrived in Yaounde with blue cloth just the right shade and texture.

Mother took the cloth to Frida, our crack seamstress who took the original shorts as a model and created a replica. On Ndi's birthday, shortly thereafter, after the proper celebration, the shorts wrapped in a bright package were given to him. No one at the party could forget the delight in Ndi's eyes when he opened the package and realized with excitement that he too owned such a splendiferous pair of shorts.

The next Sunday at church Ndi sat in his lovely blue shorts receiving the admiration and accolades of his friends. Throughout the service, he would stroke the texture of his shorts while the choirs sang their melodious renditions of hymns and while the preacher delivered the sermon. Never once was he close to dozing as were some of his friends, too proud was he of his new possessions.

A few weeks later, Ndi appeared in church wearing another pair of shorts. In his hand was a package of banana leaves tied with bush rope. Traditionally for the offering many Cameroonians brought their gifts to God in kind. When the time came Ndi went up and laid his package amid an assortment of plantains, chickens, pigs, eggs and *bibobola*.

After lunch, as usual, one of the elders came to visit my father reporting on the activities of the four church services that had taken place that day. He mentioned to Father that one of the packages contained a pair of brilliant blue shorts. Everyone knew from whom this package had come.

A bit later Mother and Dad ambled over to the home of Atangana and found Ndi with his siblings in the back yard playing an active game of African soccer, using a grapefruit for a ball. Mother beckoned to Ndi and asked him to sit with her under the huge cottonwood tree that dominated the yard. Perplexed, she asked for an explanation of his offering.

Ndi took Mother's hand and led her to a bamboo bench which Ndi's father had prepared for serious palavers and such occasions. He listened gravely while she explained the effort to which she had gone to get that material sent from the States to make into shorts for him. Her question was, "Why?"

Ndi, a lad of only eight years, attended church school regularly and there he had learned his lessons well. He looked up at her and answered, "Mama, the trousers were so beautiful and I love them dearly, but in fact I love them too much. When I wear them to church and try to worship, I can't pay attention to the words sung by the choirs nor the words of the pastor nor of scripture. So, I need to return them, in order that I can hear how to be a Christian!"

Out of the mouths of babes, often come great truths!

3

Betty and Frank Newman

How Green Was Our Christmas Tree

by Frank Newman

The year was 1949 and we were in Siangtan, an ancient town of Hunan Province in Southern China. The Communist armies had just taken over our section of the country in early November, almost without firing a shot.

Although the mission hospital staff where we worked had expected an overflow of wounded from the fighting, this had not happened for the Chinese nationalist army on learning their leader General Chiang had fled to Taiwan also left without putting up a fight. Our Chinese doctor and nurses were much relieved they had so few wounded to care for, but at the same time they felt let down by their supposed defenders.

Now Christmas approached, but it turned out to be a bleak year for Christmas tree decorations. My wife Betty and I had been in China almost ten years and stationed in Siangtan for over a year so we felt we knew our hospital and the community reasonably well. However, we did sense a growing fear in the local people about what the Communist army would do to them, and shared feelings of insecurity having heard tales from north China about what the Communist armies had done to Christians, both the Chinese and foreign missionaries, when they had captured the north.

Several weeks earlier our American embassy had flown all our fellow missionaries out of the country. As a doctor/nurse team, Betty and I had decided to stay on along with our son David. We firmly believed that the God who had protected us through several years of Japanese air raids, would again prove to be worthy of our trust, so we decided to stay with our Chinese friends through one more crisis.

Christmas was still four days away when we bought a small evergreen tree on which to hang our carefully stored ornaments. The pot-bellied stove in the corner of our living room took the chill off the room as Betty and I sat watching David and his eight-year-old Chinese playmate remove the ornaments from their boxes, admiring their glistening bright colors.

Suddenly with a loud crash, the living room door flew open. From the dark hall three masked men burst into the room, each with a gun pointed in our direction. The first strode directly toward me muttering, "I'll kill you." He stopped only when the gun was shoved against my chest. He may have pulled the trigger, but I heard no click. Only later did I realize his gun was jammed. The second man walked toward Betty while the third turned toward David. Kwang Tan, David's playmate, slipped frightened out the open door.

Taken totally by surprise, we all reacted automatically. I recall thinking of the Chinese proverb, "Never wrestle with a bullet," but automatically I pushed the gun away from my chest. Resorting to my college-developed wrestling instincts, I grappled with the gunman until we both went to the floor. By the grace of God, his gun again failed to fire.

Rising to his knees and using both hands, the gunman managed to make the gun fire, which it did with an ear splitting roar. But by this time, and again, by the grace of God, the gun was so jammed and the man's aim was so random that the bullet ricocheted around the room. After passing through a hymnbook, it came to rest in the open fireplace. For reasons I have never understood, I lay quietly on the floor so Betty — and possibly my attacker — thought I had been killed.

Meanwhile the second man had yanked at Betty's plastic beaded necklace, holding half of it in his hand as it broke. David was struggling with him when my attacker's gun went off. The tremendous noise so distracted all three of the bandits that with one accord they turned and headed for the door. As they raced down the hall toward the outside door, the third man fired a parting shot, wanting to make sure no one was following them.

In the silent darkness Betty and David stood shaking until they sensed I could stand up. Then we three embraced each other and thanked God. Miraculously, the kerosene lamp had been overturned and gone out without starting a fire. The floor was covered with fragments of Christmas tree ornaments, but we were all grateful to be alive, with nothing more serious than a shaking up. For the next four days we celebrated Christmas with a feeling of special joy and gratitude to God — even though the Christmas tree was unusually green because it had so few whole ornaments left.

The three bandits who burst into our home plus the two we learned later who accompanied them, one waiting at the outer compound gate while the other stood outside our door while the three were inside, were traced to their living quarters where the investigators found the half of Betty's pink-beaded necklace which had been torn from her neck during the melee. Using this half necklace as evidence of their guilt, the five were all found guilty by the Communist government investigators.

Hearing this, we feared we might be forced to identify them, which seemed it might mean we could be instrumental in sending them to their death. For reasons we never understood, we were not asked to identify the robbers, so were thankful for that decision. However, later we did learn these same men were convicted of making counterfeit money, a crime punishable by death.

That they were found guilty was gratifying, but that they were executed was not. Missionaries do not, as a rule, believe in capital punishment. Surely the God who gave us life is the only one wise enough to take it away. During that tumultuous Christmas season, we were glad that the strained joy of our Christmas celebration was not diminished by the knowledge that we had been asked to participate in the court proceedings that resulted in the death of five of God's creatures.

4

Esther and Bob McIntire

A Summertime Christmas

by Esther & Bob McIntire

World War II held the world in thrall in 1943 and as part of the so-called "Good Neighbor Policy" between the United States and Latin America, there was an understanding that no new Protestant missionaries would be allowed to enter the countries of South America except to replace those who retired.

Thus when a couple who served the Presbyterian Board of Foreign Missions in Buriti, Brazil — which happened to be in the exact geographical center of South America — were unable to return to the field, we were asked to replace them. Finally a cable arrived giving permission for us to labor in Brazil.

Because of wartime restrictions and submarine warfare being waged in the Atlantic, we were sent on our way by Pan American Airways but were scheduled to fly from Miami to Rio de Janeiro via the west coast of South America. We were allowed only one small suitcase for baggage, and since it was summer in the USA, we left Miami in the sweltering heat of July in rather light clothing.

It took five days of flying to finally arrive in Rio in their midwinter. Our first flight took us to tropical Panama, the next day a dawn-to-dusk flight brought us to Lima, Peru and then the next night we arrived shivering in Chile. (We soon understood why it was called "chilly"). Missionaries met us in Santiago and loaned us overcoats to wear across town over our summer clothing. The fourth day we flew over the Andes to Buenos Aires and finally our last day we journeyed to Rio de Janeiro where Presbyterian missionaries met us at the Santos Dumont airport. The winter air in Rio was cool, but the hospitality and welcome were warm.

We thought back fondly to those cool days later when we were suffering the mid-summer heat of December. By now we were settled into the Brazilian town of Lavras, Minas Gerias, huddled in the foothills of interior Brazil, with no need for heavy clothing, but plenty of requirements for adjusting to language study, a new culture, and the Brazilian way of life. Our steady diet of rice and beans was supplemented with fresh killed meat sold on the street corner, bananas grown in our backyard and corn from our garden. The baker delivered delicious, warm crusty bread to our front door and our yard produced all the oranges and tropical fruit we could eat.

There were drawbacks. The constant rain of summer, the noisy children playing in the street along with the stress of trying to communicate in a new language took their toll. Besides we were homesick. Christmas seemed hardly to be a holiday. The local shops had no sign of Santa Claus, no Christmas trees or decorations — nothing to celebrate the Season. Even the churches in this small town of Lavras held no celebration of Christ's birth.

On Christmas Eve we sat in front of our short-wave radio twirling the dials hoping to hear some sounds of Christmas. Bing Crosby crooning "I'm Dreaming of a White Christmas" would have been music to our ears, but all we heard was news of the war. Slaughter and hatred twanged through the airwaves punctuated by the constant static of summer.

Suddenly there came a loud slap on our door, then another, and another. Opening the front window, we were faced by a mob shouting in Portuguese. Our language skills were good enough to understand most of what was being said. There was no mistaking the hostility. The words "*Norteamericano*" and "*Protestante*" were rang through the air as mud balls splattered on the door and window.

Finally the jeers ceased, the crowd left, and we sat forlorn, wondering why we, who only wanted to deliver the message of love brought to the world in the birth of our Savior, should become objects of hate. Miserably, more homesick then before, we went to bed to toss and turn, wondering if we had made a big mistake in coming to this land so foreign to us.

In the darkness of the night, well before dawn, we again heard noises in front of the house. Had the mob returned to inflict bodily harm? Even death? It had happened before to missionaries here and elsewhere.

Then we heard the song of angels bidding us to fear not! "Joy to the world, the Lord is come, let earth receive her

King." The music, so familiar to us in English, was being sung with Portuguese words. We rushed to the front window, threw open the sash, raised the window high and listened as the young people from church serenaded us, just as angels had serenaded the shepherds long ago. The wife of the local pastor, seated on a donkey cart, was playing a little portable organ as the youth choir jubilantly sang to us of the birth of Jesus Christ, the Savior.

All up and down the street our neighbors came to the windows of their homes. Others came out into the street. To the young people singing carol after carol, they showed their appreciation, shouting *"Bis, Bis"* (Again, Again). And so Christmas came to that little Brazilian hill town!

Strangely, after that emotional night Lavras felt like home to us. Our neighbors now greeted us, visited with us, brought us food and made us welcome! Then a week or so later, a young man came to the door wanting to apologize for having incited that mob on Christmas Eve and asking for our forgiveness for having thrown mud on our home. His next question took us by surprise: "Will you pray with me?"

From then on he came back regularly for Bible study and prayer, becoming a firm friend. We felt anew the miracle of the Christmas carol, "All is calm! All is bright!"

We celebrated many Christmases in Brazil, but the carols of that youth choir in the early dawn of our first Christmas in the summer heat of Brazil linger with us yet. Christ's message of love, hope, and peace sung by those young carolers in the darkness before the dawn helped bring us and our new neighbors together in true friendship and community.

5

Florence Galloway and her family

Special Gifts in Cameroon

by Florence Galloway

As Christmas approached that year in Cameroon, we were living in a mud-wattle house with hard mud floors and thatched roof in Ibong. It was 1954 and we were the only missionary family in this isolated village. We'd been sent to this remote corner of the country to work in rural church building. Our predecessors had gone on furlough, so now we also were responsible for the process of completing a new residence.

Our mud-wattle house in the center of the village had been our home for over a year. A replica of everyone else's house in the village, it was so close to our neighbors we could hear them cough or talk at night—and since we spoke the local Bantu language, Basa, there were no secrets hid in our village. Daily we woke up to the sounds of the neighbor's children chattering or their babies crying. Each morning my first sight as I opened the shutters was an old grandmother who wore only a loin-cloth, with a pipe in her mouth, sweeping the front of their house with a brush-broom made of twigs bound together.

We learned a great deal more about African life than I had anticipated during that year and I was anxious for a bit of privacy. The cement house my husband Ralph had built was finally finished and I was ready to leave the leaky thatched roof with its mud floor which housed rats and snakes in its porous walls. The mud house with its shutters for windows always seemed dark and damp. Nothing seemed to dry completely from the abundant tropical rains so our shoes were moldy and our clothes were damp much of the time.

Besides these discomforts, our mud brick outdoor toilet tended to attract snakes and spiders, so I was ready for the new house with its flushing toilet plus a generator to give us electric lights in the evening to light up those dark corners instead of having to depend on the Coleman-type lamps we had.

Being seven months pregnant with our fourth child, I had added incentive to sleep in our new cement block house by Christmas Eve. Our children, aged five, three and two, were excited about moving, but also about Christmas. To help put us in the holiday mood, I had been playing Handel's "Messiah" on our battery-powered phonograph all afternoon.

By afternoon everything was packed in big cardboard boxes. The furniture had been moved to the new house, some 70 yards away from our mud house and we looked around for a last farewell before setting out. I knew Robert, three, would miss the "garages" he had tunneled for his toy cars in the mud walls. I watched carefully as our boxes were loaded on the heads of the carriers. Ralph was at the other end directing traffic as the boxes arrived at the new house. The children ran excitedly back and forth.

A young Cameroon girl was helping me make up our beds and she agreed to put some soup on for supper on our wood-burning stove. Darkness comes rapidly in the tropics and it was important to finish while there was still light, so the carriers picked up their pace and in bare feet, ran over the uneven trail in order to finish before night fell.

When it was all delivered, I sank wearily on a chair — finally in our new house. Ruthie, our oldest child, came to whisper in my ear, "Mama, where are our presents?"

"Ruthie, you know I've been too busy and haven't had time to prepare anything."

Although she knew the truth about Santa Claus, Ruthie gave me a solemn look and said, "Bonnie Jean and Robert want presents, Mama. They'll be waiting to open presents."

I shook my head, "Surely, it's enough to be in our new home."

She looked unconvinced. As the oldest of our children, she felt responsible for their welfare. Finally she suggested, "Why don't you make a cake — with white frosting. I'll make all the presents." She smiled, satisfied and happy with her solution.

So I pulled myself together and began to make a gingerbread cake, using my last cake mix which had come in a wonderful package from a church in the U.S. along with a white divinity frosting to spread generously on top of the cake. The children licked the bowl and hand egg beater.

As I was doing this Ruthie was scurrying about, finding treasurers to wrap. Several times she would ask, "May I have this?" secretly showing me something she thought was appropriate. I was glad to say, "Yes," relieved she was taking care of this project so I could get on with moving us into our new home. Bonnie Jean and Robert, sensing the excitement in the air, ran from room to room. The first thing they had tried out was the wonderful flushing toilet.

Christmas morning we sat around the breakfast table. Ruth had piled presents wrapped in old newspapers before me. "You can give them out, Mama."

There were no names. I gave a package, one at a time, to Bonnie Jean and then to Robert. Ruthie didn't want any. She didn't expect anything. She had the joy of giving.

She sat, smiling at Bonnie Jean in her high chair and Robert at the table. Both were eager to receive each present, unwrapping them with glee. There were pretty rocks, some toys of Ruthie's and the small trinkets she had picked up around the house. The children were thrilled with all the things "Santa" had brought them.

This was one of the happiest Christmases we ever had. And I had received a wonderful gift — the unexpected pleasure of seeing the love, understanding and joy of giving that had been demonstrated by our little Ruthie. Early she had learned, "It is more blessed to give than to receive."

6

Eleanor van Lierop

Yuletide Memories in Korea

by Eleanor van Lierop

Our first Christmas in Korea was a lonely time. Having been used to getting together with family during the holidays we found ourselves in a place where we had no relatives. It was even difficult to decorate for Christmas because Korean stores stocked no decorations. So we made do with our own inventions: brightly painted pine cones, amber balls wrapped in tinsel saved from a year's supply of chewing gum, strings of popcorn and streamers of interlocking paper circlets with burned-out flash bulbs painted red, green, yellow and blue.

When we had finished, though the tree did look pretty, we went to bed a bit forlorn and depressed. Suddenly in the middle of the night we were awakened by sweet music. It sounded like an angel choir! I must be dreaming, I thought snuggling deeper under the covers.

But it came again and this time I was awake enough to hear, *"Ko yohan bam, koruk han bam."* "Silent night, holy night." Springing from bed, I went to the window to investigate. It was 3 a.m. A crisp snow had fallen during the night, outlining the trees and bushes in sharp focus. And there in the cold night air was a 40-voice choir singing under our window. They followed "Silent Night" with "Hark the Herald Angels Sing," "Watchman Tell us of the Night," and then ended with "Joy to the World, the Lord has Come."

Grabbing our bathrobes, we hurried to the door to find out who they were. It turned out they had come by truck from a nearby church where they had gathered at nine to practice and memorize the words — since they couldn't read the words in the dark. After practicing, they played a few games until midnight when they stopped for a hot meal, traditionally, chicken soup filled with rice flour dumplings, called *duk kuk* and *kimchi* (spicy hot pickled cabbage).

They made it a habit to sing to shut-ins, to their pastor's family, and also to missionaries, since as one person explained, "We think missionaries are more lonesome at Christmas than any other time." They guessed right.

After thanking them heartily for their beautiful Christmas gift of music on Christmas morning, we went back to bed grateful for being given this rare treat.

An hour later we discovered it wasn't all that rare! Once more we were awakened. This time by the Yonsei University

Choir, followed shortly thereafter by the Pierson Bible Institute Band! And then by the Saemuman Presbyterian Church choir.

To each of these groups we offered our heartfelt thanks for a most beautiful, inspirational beginning of Christmas Day. It was a cherubic awakening, reminding us of that first Christmas in Bethlehem. As we crawled back to our beds, we planned to sleep the rest of the morning.

But it was not to be. An hour later our children rushed into our room crying, "Merry Christmas!" With sparkling eyes they said, "Let's go down and open our Christmas gifts!" So there was no sleeping late that morning but we cherished long the memory of the angel choirs that had announced the birthday of our Lord, just as had happened on the first Christmas morn 2,000 years ago.

One year we asked the Saemuman Church choir if we could accompany them. It was a bit difficult to memorize all the words of the carols in Korean, so we brought flashlights as props—even though this was expressly forbidden as it would destroy the hallowed atmosphere they wanted to create. What fun it was visiting, playing games and eating *duk kuk*. Soon we climbed aboard trucks to make our visit around town, singing, "Joy to the world, the Lord is come." We tried hard to remember all the words so we wouldn't wreck the mood.

Years later, we had harsher memories from our Christmas. Our four children were in America attending college, and even though we were alone, we decorated the tree and house for the holidays as usual. Under the tree we placed the Christmas gifts sent by our children, parents, relatives and friends. What a colorful sight they made in their variety of Yuletide wrappings.

After a gala dinner on Christmas Eve, we went to visit an orphanage to bring Christmas gifts for everyone as well as treats of Christmas cookies and candy. After the presents, we sang Christmas carols together, read the Christmas story from the Bible and told some other Christmas stories. In turn, the young people from the orphanage dramatized the story for us in a most realistic way.

It was a splendid evening and we returned home exhausted from all the excitement, ready to turn in. Arriving home, we were surprised to see the large double front doors of our house wide open. We had left them closed and locked. What had happened? Rushing in we found all our presents under the Christmas tree had disappeared. Instead there was a string of name tags, Christmas cards and letters which led from our house down the path to the road. Thieves had visited us while we were away and taken everything!

Of course there were tears as we thought about the gifts of love from our children and family which we were never to see, but then the joy of our Christmas Eve with the Korean children came to mind. After all, Christmas is really in the heart, not under the tree. God had given us a chance to make sure we remembered this truth!

Another memorable Christmas scene began in the fellowship hall as the Christmas drama was unfolding. Mary exhausted, lying on a bed of straw, cradled her newborn son on her arm. Joseph concerned himself with a group of shepherds who had entered the stable yard speaking of the angels who had appeared to them saying, "Go to Bethlehem and see the child born to be King and Savior of the world!"

A hush surrounded the tableau, as the audience watched the actors, lost in the real meaning of the nativity story. Suddenly a piercing cry broke the silence followed by loud sobs of deep grief. The voice cried out, "I sorry! I sorry!"

I wormed my way through the packed hall to see the cause of this outburst. There was Sun Ok on her knees before the Christ-child, worshipping in deep penitence. "What can I give him?" she sobbed. "I no money, I no things. I nothing to give Jesus. I give me!"

When she saw me beside her she turned, still weeping and repeating her remarkable offering, "I no nothing. I work hard for you. I good worker, I work hard for Jesus."

Gently pulling Sun Ok to her feet, I guided her into an adjacent room where she could explain. The other girls had brought gifts to lay under the Christmas tree — simple things they had made or bought with meager earnings: aprons, socks, mittens, combs, barrettes, broaches. All these would go to a nearby orphanage.

Sun Ok who had been admitted to the Girls' Welfare Association barely a month before had nothing ready to give. But she had caught the real Christmas message and responded wholeheartedly. God wants such gifts — alive, loving, understanding, comforting, joyful, thankful bodies. Only weeks before Sun Ok had been a prostitute!

She had come in early December, 19 years old, with glossy black hair, smiling eyes and round cheeks that blushed readily. Of medium stature, with a slight body, she had been referred by the YWCA who operated a trade school in tailoring for widows and jobless girls. When it was discovered she had been a street girl, she was sent to the Girls' Welfare Association for special help.

Sun Ok remained faithful to her Christmas promise. She committed herself to God and wanted to stay on at the House of Grace as a helper or aide. Our staff warned her not to overlook what might be the chance of her lifetime: becoming a teacher in a dressmaking school, but Sun Ok was adamant. She had made a promise which she must keep. So she worked diligently cleaning, washing, ironing, gardening, cheering, praising and joking along with the other girls to get them to put forth their best efforts.

A year later a pastor wrote that his church wanted to grant a scholarship to a girl who had a middle school education enabling her to attend the Bible institute. When we looked around, Sun Ok seemed the ideal person. She had developed into a wise, responsible and caring person with just enough independence to persevere in this kind of training.

Selfishly we hated to lose her but were glad for this opportunity which, it seemed, God had given her. When she finished her schooling, she became a paid church worker in a country church — a Bible woman as they are called in Korea. These women act much like assistant ministers for they go calling with the pastor and supervise the ministry with the women and children of the church. For me, Sun Ok's ministry was always a reminder of a most memorable Christmas.

7

Marabelle Taylor with African friends

Joy from Simple Christmas Presents

by J. Lawrence Driskill

"How did you get so many boils all over your body?" asked missionary nurse Marabelle Taylor.

"The doctor says it was caused by malnutrition," replied the missionary mother.

"You mean you haven't been getting enough food?" asked Marabelle in a shocked voice. "I know some of our African patients are malnourished. They don't understand nutrition and poverty drags them down. But how did it happen to you?"

In an almost apologetic voice the missionary replied, "You know this terrible World War II is eating up the world's resources and because of the war, it is hard to send money from America to Africa. The Americans who support our work aren't able to send us much now and by the time I feed my husband and two children, I guess I forget to eat enough nourishing food to keep myself healthy. That's why a friend had to bring me to your hospital here in Elat from our missionary work far away in a remote village."

"Who is taking care of your children while you are in the hospital?" asked Marabelle.

"My husband is caring for them right here on the hospital grounds," replied the mother. "Your administrator kindly let them stay in your 'Missionary Annex' and even helped to buy food for them. I am grateful."

"Have you made any Christmas plans for your children?" asked Marabelle.

"No," answered the mother. "These have been pretty lean years, and we never seem to have enough money to do much at Christmas. Usually we give each of the children a bar of scented soap, but this year my nine-year-old daughter is begging for a doll. She has never had one."

"Maybe I can help," said Marabelle. "We have received a couple of barrels filled with good used clothing and nice toys to share with the missionary community and our African neighbors. Maybe I can find a doll for your little girl. I can't promise until I look, but I assure you they can share in the annual Christmas party we are giving. Because of the war most of our children had to go back to America. It will be good to have your children with us this Christmas."

Marabelle began her search. She found a lovely toy car and

truck for the seven-year-old boy and, finally, she located a beautiful doll — just right for the little girl.

At that time Marabelle was a nurse in the mission hospital at Elat in Cameroon, Africa. This large hospital took care of 1,500 leprosy patients in separate compounds and some 150 sick people at the hospital. Usually there were also many missionary children attending the school on the hospital grounds — some from families who served at the hospital and others from far away who lived in a school dormitory.

Each Christmas there was a joyful holiday dinner planned in the dining hall of the school. Now since the war had forced many children to stay in America, Marabelle was especially glad these two children could share in the Christmas celebration and brighten the celebration by their presence.

Marabelle loved children so much that later on after the war, she dedicated herself to saving the lives of almost 400 African babies whose mothers died in childbirth or who were abandoned for other reasons. For over 20 years Marabelle cared for them in her home, giving them love and attention.

When the Christmas celebration came that year Marabelle enjoyed the pageant, the Christmas carols and the fellowship, but was looking forward to the time the children would be opening their gifts. She especially wanted to see how the missionary's young daughter would respond to her first doll.

Marabelle recalled later, "When that precious little girl opened that package and saw the doll, her whole face lit up with surprise and joy. She literally shook with excitement as she cradled the doll in her arms, holding it tight all evening — never wanting to put it down.

"Watching her delight, my thoughts went back to that first Christmas at Bethlehem. I could imagine Mary holding the

Baby Jesus in her arms with that same jubilation and thanksgiving. Surely the Christmas love and joy that was born with Jesus had now come alive in the heart of this young girl."

Reflecting on how little it takes to cheer the heart of someone who has so little, Marabelle recalled, "Years after this I learned that my African Christian friends could rejoice at receiving even smaller Christmas treats. Once when I was operating a mobile clinic in the remote Babimbi Hills I celebrated Christmas with some 150 African friends. Their diet was so limited they ate meat only once or twice a month. Even then it was usually a kind of meat most of us would not want — mostly monkeys, snakes or lizards. Of course Christmas treats like candy, cakes and mixed nuts were unknown."

So Marabelle decided that as a "Christmas treat" she was going to try to get one whole sardine for each person in the village. They loved the tasty and nutritious sardines — but in order to get enough fish for all 150 in the village, Marabelle had to travel to a distant market and buy large cans of them — which she proceeded to do.

The village was thrilled and in response they put on quite an impressive Christmas program — a three-hour production of singing, preaching plus a marvelous Christmas play. There was an adult choir, a children's choir and group singing — and each sang several times. To help with the music, they swayed with their bodies and clapped their hands in time, putting every fiber of their beings into this Christmas celebration.

All this to celebrate the present of one sardine per villager!

Such a simple gift made these people, who had so little, joyful and thankful at Christmas. Their joy was enhanced by the love born in Bethlehem — God's gift to the whole world.

8

Nick and Rhoda Iyoya

A Lonely Christmas Eve in Japan

by **Nicholas M. Iyoya**

I felt much alone that Christmas Eve in 1982 in Iwakuni, Japan. Sitting in my office at the Community Center located just outside the U.S. Marine Air Base which shared an air strip with the Japanese Self Defense Force, I stared out my window watching the icy snow flurries as they beat against the pane.

My wife Rhoda was in California with our children. Just a

little over a month before we had been summoned on an emergency back to the States to arrange for the funeral of our 21-year-old son who had been in his senior year at Vassar College and had taken his own life. After the funeral I returned to Japan to resume my duties as missionary to the Kyodan, or the United Church of Christ in Japan, and director of the Community Center serving U.S. Marine personnel. Rhoda had stayed on in the States with our children for several months and was planning to rejoin me in Japan in March.

Thus I had no prospect for being with family. It would be my first Christmas Eve all by myself. As the evening wore on, I was feeling increasingly forlorn. Unlike other nights, scarcely anyone passed by our building. Perhaps it was the snow storm or it might have been because it was Christmas Eve. Most of the marines seemed to have returned to the base and the Japanese appeared to have stayed home.

My thoughts raced across the Pacific to my family. I wondered what Rhoda and the children were thinking and feeling at that moment. The more I pondered my family's situation, the more intensely I felt the pangs of solitude and sadness. In the midst of this unhappy scene, a ray of light beamed. It turned out to be the headlights of a car shining directly at my front office window.

Out in the dark night I heard voices. Moments later a bus parked in front of our building and some 20 people alighted holding flashlights. Quickly I went out to see who these night visitors might be. They turned out to be caroling friends from the Higashi Church in Iwakuni come to sing the ever familiar tunes of "The First Noel," "It Came Upon a Midnight Clear," and "Silent Night." As the strains filled the cold night air, I stood in speechless wonder with tears streaming down my face.

At a loss for words, all I could say was "Thank you, thank you." A warmth went through me as I realized I was not alone after all. In place of my family, whom I missed terribly, here was God's gift of an extended family surrounding me with their love and their songs. I thought about the words of our Lord: "There is no one who has left house, brothers or children ... for my sake, who will not receive a hundred fold now — brothers and sisters, mothers and children ..." (Mk 10:29-30).

Truly, I was not alone after all. Never will I forget that snowy Christmas Eve in Japan.

Editors Note: Nicholas (Nick) Iyoya was not the only one deeply affected by the death of his son John. At Vassar, John's love for children and his dedicated community service won him many admirers. Below is a description of a memorial to John:

> John's classmates and the Department of Education at Vassar College have established as a memorial to John an annual week-long Children's Art Show at Vassar College during which time the art work of the children of the Poughkeepsie schools is shown. The "John Iyoya Prize" is awarded at that time by the Department of Education to the student who most exemplified John's love for children and their art in their student teaching.

9

Clara Lindholm and family

Christmas in Occupied Philippines

by Clara Lindholm

We were teaching in the Divinity School at Silliman University on the Philippine island of Negros when the Japanese military invaded the Philippines that December 1941. Soon the school authorities decided we needed to be evacuated away from our vulnerable seaside location to a hiding place deep in the island's mountainous interior.

Christian Malahay, one of our students at Silliman, escorted us to the hinterland where his father owned farmland. There his family kept us hidden, fed us and advised us when to move higher up in the mountains. At Christmastime we were still refugees, cut off from the outside world.

We had four children, the youngest just born the day the Japanese attacked Pearl Harbor. It was the memories of other Christmases, when life was normal, that made our jungle plight seem worse than it actually was. We were living in a dwelling built of split bamboo, up on stilts. It was some fifteen by ten feet rectangular with walls woven from narrow strips of tropical leaves. We called it our "wicker basket."

That fact made it easy to arrange old Christmas cards along the walls, securing them between the slats. Sent by family and friends from the U.S. the year before, these cards helped to bridge the distance to our far away loved ones. On one wall we put together a crude creche inside an old dry milk box.

For presents the children made their father some lengths of cord by twisting abaca fibers (known as "Manila Hemp") together. For me there was a small basket woven out of narrow strips of coconut palm-leaf. With some instruction from our new rural friends, we managed to craft bamboo whistles for the boys, a riding-horse from a large banana plant stalk for Beverly and a stocking-doll for the baby.

On Christmas we sat in our simple hut exchanging gifts, baby Janet asleep on a grass mat on the floor. Every time she woke up, one of the other children would hurry to pick her up and cuddle her. I mused on how blessed we really were, in spite of outward appearances. Our children were happy, playful and healthy. We were all together as a family surrounded by loving and caring Filipino friends nearby. The Lord our God was with

us and we had Jesus' promise: "Lo, I am with you always ..."
It almost seemed as if it could be a normal Christmas.

Suddenly my husband Paul said, "Wouldn't it be great if we could somehow fix up a Christmas tree for the children?"

"There are lots of trees in the forest, but you know evergreens don't grow here." I replied.

"In any case," Paul continued, "I'm going to ask a neighbor to go with me to see what we can find."

Soon they ventured into the forest where they were surrounded by towering *luan* trees and *bagtic* trees — whose sap is used to make torches. As they searched for a suitable "Christmas" tree, monkeys scampered along on their elevated tree-top trails chattering and scolding the trespassers.

They passed the cave where our family had retreated on several occasions when danger from enemy patrols had been feared. Here we had survived for weeks. A split-bamboo floor had been anchored to the stalagmites, giving us a place to lie down. A ceiling made from over-lapping banana leaves was stretched over us to keep the dripping stalactites from getting us wet and dirty. Each day a deacon brought us food and water and caribou milk for the baby.

Suddenly the searching men came upon a bed of ferns with sturdy stalks which somehow resembled cedar tree branches. Paul got an idea. "Why don't we find a small pyramidal-shaped tree, strip off its leaves and in their place tie these ferns onto the bare branches. Thus was our Christmas tree born.

When it was set up, this invention delighted the children who proceeded to decorate it with lovely red hibiscus blossoms, hanging them upside down to look like bells. A piece of tinfoil became a star for the top of the tree. "Candy canes" made with paper striped with red crayons and stuffed with cotton added an imaginary sweet touch. Bits of white cotton snowflakes tipped the branches.

Then it was time for our shared Christmas celebration with our Filipino protectors and friends. These were all doing subsistence farming in this remote area and had a Sunday school where each week they gathered in the largest dwelling in the area for a Bible study and worship service. Once a month as many as could walked down to the lowland where they worshiped at an established church with an ordained pastor and where they could take communion.

Osias Montejar, a deacon of our little mountain group, had recently built the small bamboo dwelling in which we were living. He intended it for his family, but to accommodate us he had moved his family back into their former ramshackle building which had been used as a corncrib. The sacrifice of his family on our behalf touched us deeply.

For Christmas everyone crowded into the community gathering place so the program could begin. A long-time unused lantern was brought out to light up the simple drama depicting the nativity story. The eager and appreciative congregation looked on as the drama coach lead the actors through their paces. Between each scene he turned down the lantern wick to conserve fuel. As one scene led to the next, the coach would ask one or another in the audience to loan a coat or a shawl needed for an upcoming part. Even though it was a bit impromptu, everyone thoroughly enjoyed this dramatization of the story of Jesus' birth.

After the drama it was our turn to share and so we told them about celebrating Christmas in America where we gathered around a Christmas tree, an "evergreen" that stayed green all year — symbolizing the everlasting life Christ came to bring to everyone. The star that sat on the top of the Christmas tree represented the star which led the Magi to the Christ child — the Light of the World and the Prince of Peace.

After this we sang Christmas carols together and exchanged joyful Christmas greetings. As we walked back to our humble dwelling in the moonlight, to surroundings so different from any we had ever known, we thanked God for these dear people. We gave thanks for their devotion to the Lord, for their unselfish acts of hospitality, and their enduring loyalty and love. All in all it was one of our happiest Christmases ever.

10

Millie Brown and her Japanese coworkers

Japan's "Christmas School"

by **Mildred R. Brown**

One could almost call it the "Christmas School." Japan's North Star School (*Hokusei Gakuen*) was founded in 1887 by Sarah Smith, a courageous missionary who when ordered to return home for health reasons by the Presbyterian Board of Foreign Missions went instead to Hokkaido, Japan's northern island — which at the time was a cold, undeveloped wilderness.

43

In the frontier town of Sapporo she rented a stable and there established the town's first girls' school. *Hokusei* alumnae like to point out that their North Star School, whose motto is, "Shine like stars in a dark world," was born in a stable.

I arrived in *Hokusei* in the fall of 1953. A month later, while I was teaching a class, I was surprised to hear the "Hallelujah Chorus" being sung down the hall. Although it was only October, all the teachers were talking about the Christmas worship service. As a new teacher, I was surprised to be asked to take charge of the sheep for the Nativity pageant.

Actually the "sheep" turned out to be the smallest first year junior high girls who were to wear long white underwear, white socks, mittens and stocking caps with little ears sewn on them. They were to crawl onto the stage during the shepherd scene and later accompany the shepherds to the manger.

It had already turned cold, but in 1953 the school could not afford to turn the heat on until December, so every day after school the cast practiced in a frigid auditorium. Each rehearsal was opened with prayer because the drama coach wanted to emphasize that this pageant was to be our gift to the Baby Jesus, and for that reason it had to be as beautiful as possible. It was thrilling to participate in the preparations and watch the joy of my little sheep who had heard the Christmas story that year for the first time.

By the middle of November we had already had eight inches of beautiful snowfall — but even that didn't change the timetable for putting on any heat in the buildings. I was the weakling who put on my snowsuit every day as soon as classes finished before heading to the auditorium. The "sheep" practiced in their coats and slacks.

Soon we were singing Christmas carols every day in the

morning chapel service and staying afterward to practice more carols or the "Hallelujah Chorus." Finally the long awaited first day of December arrived. Even with the joyous heat turned on, I found we still needed lots of warm clothing, but at least now we no longer saw our breath in the classrooms. My anticipation of warmth was short-lived, however, because the minute classes were over, the heat went off, so the cold rehearsals continued.

I was unprepared for the many invitations that started pouring in, all written on handmade cards decorated with original drawings: "Please come to our homeroom Christmas party ..." There were dozens of parties — all following the time-honored *Hokusei* pattern: A choir processed in singing "O Come, All Ye Faithful" followed by a worship service led by the students. Then came a nativity pageant and finally the food and perhaps a gift exchange. Usually two or three students gave speeches.

I'll never forget one made by a little first year junior high girl, Junko: "This is the most wonderful Christmas I have ever had. At home we always ate decorated cake at Christmas which I really like, but now I know what Christmas really *means*."

Finally the day for the Christmas worship service arrived. It was snowing — Sapporo always seems to have a white Christmas. The junior high service was to be given in the morning, the senior high in the afternoon, with a combination of the two in the evening for parents and the public.

The snow was deep by the time the evening service started, but that didn't keep anyone away. Long before the curtain went up, the chapel was completely filled with families, friends and alumnae. When the candle light processional entered, the dingy old chapel was illuminated by the light of hundreds of tiny "stars."

It was all splendid. The little white sheep all remembered

their places when they crawled onto the stage to worship the Baby Jesus. No one in the audience was aware the choirs sang one verse of "We Three Kings of Orient Are" three times because one of the Magi had fainted just before "he" was to enter and quickly had to be substituted.

At last everyone rose for the singing of the "Hallelujah Chorus." After the benediction people gathered around the big tree in the lobby to sing carols and then the guests went to the various classrooms for Japanese tea, rice cakes and tangerines. Exclamations of joy filled the air when mothers met former classmates whom they had not seen since last year's *Hokusei* Christmas.

As the guests reluctantly began to start home, they stepped out into a transformed world of pure white. The snow was still falling and the trees and shrubs were bending under its weight as though they too were worshiping the Christ child.

Long before dawn the next morning, Dorothy Taylor and I were awakened by the dorm students singing carols beneath our bedroom windows: *"Morobito ..."* "Joy to the world, the Lord is come!"

In the midst of the group stood little Junko, her face radiating the joy she had so recently put into words: "Now I know what Christmas really *means*."

11

Joseph Gray

Navajo Christmas Celebrations

by Joseph Gray

By the time I arrived in 1953 to work among the Navajos on their reservation in Chinle, Arizona there had been a Presbyterian church there for 29 years, ever since Pastor and Mrs. Charles Bysegger had come as missionaries to this place.

Their first Christmas, the Byseggers put on a program that attracted a full church even though Chinle was a tiny government settlement of less than 200 people most of whom worked at the boarding school, the offices of the Bureau of Indian Affairs, the two trading posts or the public health clinic in town.

For this special holiday program, people crowded in from the many sheep camps in the area.

However the "peace and goodwill" which the angels announced at Jesus' birth was in short supply because of tensions between the Roman Catholics and the Protestants in town. The Catholic mission had been established in tiny Chinle first and its priests felt there was no need for another church in town. But since the Presbyterians had a brand new building, the curious Navajos flocked to the new building — the women and girls in their long, brightly colored skirts and blouses, the men and boys in their boots and cowboy hats which they wore indoors and out.

The program was quite simple. After singing "Joy to the World," the boarding school children spoke their pieces and then an elder speaking in Navajo told the story of the birthday of our Lord. Pastor Bysegger, speaking through an interpreter, invited those who wished to give Christ room in their hearts to raise their hand.

Silence was his response, until a Navajo man spoke up, "We have no room; we are too sleepy!" His rejoinder was not surprising since Navajos tended to go to bed with the sun in those days. So after Mrs. Bysegger sang "No Room in the Inn," candy was given to everyone and the party was over.

Later the Byseggers found out there had been a subsequent gathering that same night where the tribal leaders discussed the rivalry between the Protestants and the Catholics. One man who supported the "Short-coats" (Protestant missionaries) told the group, "I came very near saying I will give Christ room in my heart and hogan."

When we arrived in Chinle fortunately the internecine rivalry had ended. In fact the first person to call on us was the

Catholic priest come to welcome us. Fortunately for us Pastor Bysegger had refused to fight the priests. Since he had been called to serve a small group of Protestants who had been led to Christ by missionaries traveling on horseback from neighboring missions, he began with a small nucleus of believers who wanted services compatible with what they had come to expect from their experience with the itinerant preachers.

The Byseggers had worked faithfully among the Navajos for many years, showing kindness to the sick, visiting those in hospitals, lending a helping hand to their neighbors to improve their living conditions, and in general winning the goodwill of many in the tribe. The priests also concluded it was more Christ-like to cooperate than be contentious.

We also found when we arrived, the Yuletide celebrations had become so popular throughout the tribe, Christmas trees were common and gift giving was an integral part of the holiday season. Also everyone had come to expect wonderful gift bundles handed out at the Presbyterian church each Christmas.

These took a whole month's time to put together by a group of half a dozen women including my wife. Hundreds of gifts had to be sorted and placed in appropriate bundles. These came each year from churches and women's societies all over the country. The sorting was essential, for no boy must receive a girl's doll and no girl receive a boy's toy! Each bundle had the family's name on the blanket in which it was wrapped.

At the end of the Christmas program, those who could read English would help distribute bundles to the wife and children, stepping gingerly between all the families sitting on the floor. The benches in the church would have been removed to allow over a hundred families to crowd into the room. The men mostly stood outside the open doors.

My first Christmas in Chinle, the elders explained that we needed to arrange for a Navajo policeman to attend to handle the intoxicated men and overly eager women and children who charged the door to get their candy and fruit. In the past some children had been hurt in the crush of the mob. Since this seemed hardly in keeping with a Christmas celebration, I proposed the elders handle any intoxicated men and I would take care of the crowd inside. By explaining what needed to happen to avoid any difficulty, I easily got everyone's cooperation and we had a wonderful celebration—which over the next two decades only got bigger each year.

People eagerly looked forward to the Christmas programs which became a focal point of the community's life together. After Christmas carols were sung in Navajo, there would be a manger scene pageant put on by the costumed children followed by a short sermon reminding us all of why we give gifts at Christmas.

The gifts we distributed to everyone afterwards were a tangible message that their Christian neighbors cared about the Navajo people. Like God's love, who had made a gift of his son to become the Savior of all of us, so Christians were expressing their love for God by sending them gifts of clothes, toys and other useful items. Thus it was, throughout our years of ministry with the Navajos, Christmas continued to be a high point of the Christian year for the believers.

12

Thelma Appleton and Filipino Christmas Star

Maayong Pasko in the Philippines

by **Thelma Appleton**

Even after 21 years of living in the Philippines, it was hard to equate our hot, sticky humidity with Christmas. But with time we learned to accept the south-of-the-equator/mid-summer heat and say *"Maayong Pasko"* or "Merry Christmas" with the genuine spirit of the Holy Season.

Our first Christmas in the Philippines, 1936, we were a young couple with a two-year old son living in Dumaguete. Wanting to retain some of our own family traditions, we planned a family Christmas that would at least remind us of "home." Donnie was old enough to catch the holiday fervor and he had heard about "Santa Claus" so he kept asking if Santa were coming and if we would have a Christmas tree.

In this lush country, that seemed easy enough, so we assured him, "Of course, we will," not realizing how difficult it would turn out to be in this tropical town. Missionary friends pointed us in the direction of the town market where the Filipinos offered a pretty sad imitation Christmas tree made out of what looked like hemp bottle brushes dyed green. Finally we landed in the Japanese Bazaar where we bought an artificial tree that at least looked somewhat real. This sufficed for several successive Yuletide holidays.

Then came the wonderful year when we were fortunate enough to get a real tree from the mountains. What a thrill to have the pungent fragrance of pine wafting through the house. From then on we tried to get real trees to hold up our Christmas decorations.

Through the years we found a diversity of trees to grace our home during the holidays: There was the swamp tree with fringed green crepe paper on its branches or the foil tree which reflected the colored lights. Best of all was the potted palmera. When lights and colored balls were hung on its branches, it turned out to be the favorite tropical substitute for our "Christmas in the land of the palm tree and vine."

Of course the Filipinos had their own Christmas traditions which were more suitable to the heat and humidity of the area. Our first Christmas, walking down the street I saw friends hanging a big paper-covered star in the front of their doorway. When we asked what it was for, our friends explained, "It's called a *Parol* and everyone has at least one every Christmas.

It's the most typical decoration of the season for us."

They added, "The star is made of split bamboo put together like a kite, with two sides tied at the corners and smaller bamboo sticks in the center to hold the two sides apart so that a candle or electric light can be placed in the center. *Parols* are covered with bright-colored paper to make them beautiful. Some are more elaborate and attractive than others and often there are contests to determine the most distinctive creation."

They were so attractive, I was determined we had to make one ourselves. A friend showed the procedures and from then on we made one every year. These star lanterns are always hung in the windows or doorways to symbolize the welcome the family has prepared for the Holy Family. They are also left hanging outside for weeks after January sixth, the "Three Kings Day" which is the traditional gift-giving day in the Philippines.

I learned about another Philippine Christmas custom once when I was visiting a Filipina neighbor. "Why do you have banana trees growing on your porch?" I asked her.

"Oh, they're not growing here," she replied. "We cut them from our garden and tie them to the posts. When the fruit is ripe, it is a signal to our friends and neighbors the time has come for a festive celebration where we share the fruits of the farm. This year you and your family must come to our party."

Another Christmas convention we came to look forward to were the roving musical bands, called *comparsas,* that visited all the homes in town to play Filipino folk songs and carols. For this they expected a small monetary gift. Children from the country would also come singing, with visions of a few centavos for their efforts dancing in their wee heads.

During our first Christmas season I was awakened one night by a series of loud bangs. Frightened, I asked my husband

"What's that noise?" He assured me it was only the sound of firecrackers. Thus we discovered that firecrackers and big bamboo cannon are equally to be expected as part of Christmas and New Year celebrations. In fact, during the holiday when you walked the streets downtown in Dumaguete, you had to be careful and learn to dodge the fireworks.

Throughout the Yuletide Season, there was lovely Christmas music on every hand. For me the most impressive always was listening to Handel's "Messiah" sung by the hundred-voice student choir at the Silliman University Church. Since practice for this started in late October, it was a treat to live in a house nearby where the strains of this beautiful music would float by for weeks before the final performance. We never tired of it — even the practice sessions.

There was no air mail service during the first years of our life in the Philippines, so our Christmas cards and packages tended to arrive in late January or February. This turned out to be a wonderful way to extend the holiday. Since we were so far away from home, it was always a joy to receive messages from family and friends. Being separated from them was always the most difficult during Christmas.

However holiday time in the Philippines was a joyous occasion for our family as we celebrated the birth of the Christ child with our many new friends — and their varied customs. In time we learned to appreciate the true meaning of Merry Christmas or *Maayong Pasko* in a foreign land.

13

Kenn and Sue Carmichael

The News for Bethlehem Shepherds

by Sue & Kenn Carmichael

During the years we served the church in Jerusalem and the Middle East, we heard many dramatizations of the Christmas narrative. Here is one about the shepherds' role that we always enjoyed.

On a hill that overlooked the town, two figures sat on either side of an open fire. "Perhaps," said the larger one, "if I had been born in an earlier generation and in a fine family, I would have risen to a position of great importance in the synagogue, even in the temple ... as high priest."

The speaker was a giant of a man, with a face browned by the sun and the wind. He struck the palm of his hand with a great fist. "Tending sheep! Me! When I might have been born to become at the very least a rabbi!"

His companion smiled, saying nothing. Much smaller than the other, he was scarcely more than a child. Leaning forward, his chin cupped in his hands, he gazed intently into the fire.

The big man spoke again. "Are you warm enough, lad?"

"Yes, Uncle," he replied, tucking the rug about his legs.

His uncle continued, "Or I might have been born much later, say, at the time of the Messiah. That would be glory for you! To serve both God and the Savior of Israel at the same time, in the same temple ... oh that I could see the day!"

Lifting his gaze skyward, he said, "Ezra, see that star that seems to be suspended directly over the town? Look how much brighter and bigger it is than all the rest. That's what I would have liked to have been — something greater and more glorious than just a lowly shepherd." He turned to the silent figure across from him. "What do you say, Ezra? Come, we must talk or else take turns sleeping. Do you prefer to sleep?"

"But think, Uncle," replied the lad, "if you'd been born earlier or in the far future, I'd have missed your company."

Aaron grunted. "I know. Even Father used to say I dreamt too much of what might have been or of what shall come."

"No, Uncle, don't misunderstand me." Ezra was still smiling. "It's not that you dream too much. Heaven knows I do my share of dreaming. It's just that ... Well ... "

"Out with it, young one. I'm big enough to take criticism, I think. At least from you."

"I don't mean to criticize, Uncle. It's just I wish you could be content. I know herding sheep is nobody's idea of an exalted life. And I agree with you there's also danger in too much contentment. Things aren't perfect, of course."

"That's the point," replied Aaron. "If only the rest of the

family would see it. I don't expect things to be perfect but I'd like to be in a position where I could help make them so."

Ezra nodded his head slowly. "It's a worthy goal, Uncle Aaron. But could you do that best in the temple?"

"Of course I could. Where better? Certainly not in this business." Aaron got to his feet and looked scornfully about him. "Shepherding a flock of dumb animals by day and nursing them by night! How can you serve God in this forsaken spot?"

Before Ezra could reply, a voice hailed them from a distance. "Aaron! Ezra!" Running feet were heard before the owner of the feet ran breathlessly into the circle of light.

Aaron exclaimed, "Jerial, good cousin, take it easy. You'll lose that precious fat you've been saving for the next famine!"

"There's no time for jesting," panted the newcomer. "Listen closely, for I can stay but a moment." He proceeded to tell them the news about a glorious event that had just happened in a nearby field. Astonishingly a heavenly host had appeared before a group of humble shepherds to announce the birth of the Messiah. Jerial added that Malachi and three others had offered to stay behind to watch the family flocks while the rest went up to Bethlehem. Then barely catching his breath, Jerial sped into the darkness to tell others the good news.

After a shocked second, Ezra cried, "Uncle, don't you see? This means you've lived neither too soon nor too late. The Messiah has just been born so your dreams have come true!"

Aaron didn't respond immediately. His great hands were clenched tightly at his side and his mouth was set in an unforgiving line. Angry tears welled from his eyes. Finally he muttered, "Bethlehem ... in a stable ... our Redeemer, a child of the common people!" Raising his arms skyward, he cried,"My God, how can you have done this?" Then flinging himself to his knees, the great man buried his face in his hands sobbing.

"Uncle," Ezra lamented, "Don't break your heart over this. Perhaps God is trying to teach us a lesson. Maybe it has happened this way so we will learn not to exalt ourselves, but to serve God humbly wherever we may find ourselves."

Aaron slowly raised his head. "Is it wrong, then, to want to serve the Lord in the temple and be a great preacher?"

"No, it cannot be wrong, Uncle. Perhaps it all depends upon whether we want to serve the Lord or only ourselves."

Aaron looked at the young lad sharply. Then his face softened and a trace of a smile could be seen as he wiped his eyes. "How can I be angry with you? You've spoken the truth."

Ezra looked at him with bright eyes, "Come, Uncle. Let's leave our sheep with Malachi and go to town with the others."

Aaron rose to his feet and walked around the fire. "All right, lad. Up you go!" Removing the rug from around the boy's legs, he stooped to lift him gently to his shoulders.

As the tall figure started off toward the village, Ezra spoke softly in his uncle's ear, "Uncle, do you know what I dream about? I dream someday my legs will no longer be weak and crooked, but straight and strong like yours. So strong that I can carry you wherever you want to go, just as you carry me."

The big man laughed. "Then, my boy, what would there be left for me to do on this earth?"

"For one thing," said Ezra, "you could spend all your time becoming a high priest in the temple."

Aaron laughed loudly. Then he looked up beyond the slope where the star hung over the town. A great joy filled his heart and he grasped the legs of little Ezra more tightly as the two of them sped up the hill toward Bethlehem.

14

Bob and Anna Caldwell

The Hotheaded Preacher's Christmas

by Robert Caldwell

There may be occasional preachers who "set their churches on fire," plus some who cause a few raised eyebrows. Here is a tale of a preacher who kept a church from catching on fire, but lost some eyebrows in the attempt.

It happened at the annual Christmas party for the Sunday school, with the run-of-the-mill cute, albeit predictable, Christmas pageant. A lighted Christmas tree was the centerpiece of the drama — a tree lighted, unwisely, by candles. As soon as I heard about the plans, I had protested the candles but older and wiser heads had assured me it had been done before without incident. Since I was serving my first church, I was still being cautious about making changes. Perhaps it was in keeping with the spirit of Christmas, in any case I thought it wiser to keep the peace and so let it go.

The pageant progressed creakingly. Everything went more or less well until an overly enthusiastic ten-year old lad in a shepherd's garb bumped into the table holding the lit tree. That was all that was needed! A candle tipped and the tree blazed.

Fire! Fire! The cry was raised and (this was 55 years ago) I leapt onto the platform, seized the tree by the base. Holding it at arms length, I ran across the platform through the door leading to the study and then outside, tossing it into the snow.

Applause greeted my return, but when I took my seat I smelled singed hair. My hands seemed pinker than usual — and hairless — and later I realized my eyebrows were missing.

I also had to suffer through quite a few digs; "Preacher, we never knew you could move so fast," etc. Even an elder chimed in, "Now we'll be known as the church with the hotheaded preacher!"

That evening the Christmas Spirit of love and joy prevailed, so we overcame that exciting distraction and went on to complete the Christmas pageant without further trouble. We ended with "Joy to the World, the Lord is come" and even the smell of singed eyebrows didn't keep me from enjoying the fellowship and refreshments with rejoicing church members.

Later, I even lived down the corny jokes about being the "hotheaded" preacher. Eventually fresh eyebrows grew where my singed stumps had been and I went on to help prepare and enjoy many Christmas celebrations over the many years of my ministry — but none with lighted candles on a tree.

15

Nannie Hereford

Celebrating Christmas in Japan

by Nannie Hereford

It might seem strange to live in a country where Christmas is not a legal holiday, but Japan — where I was born and later served as a missionary for 33 years — is such a country. Even though now Japanese department stores have elaborate Christmas decorations and play holiday music, everyone is expected to go to work as usual on Christmas Day.

The biggest holiday of the year in Japan is New Year's Day. In fact their celebration lasts five days with stores and banks closed tight. Christmas is a new holiday for Japan and they have taken over only the commercial aspects of it. To accommodate its being a work day, Christian churches tend to celebrate by having their children's programs the Sunday before. And since many Christians are the only one from their family who are Christians, churches in Japan tend to have parties on Christmas so everyone has a place to celebrate. This might be a simple supper followed by a more elaborate tea and cakes or a full dinner similar to what we expect in the U.S. Each church tends to develop its own traditions for Christmas.

When I was teaching in a mission school in the 30s, most students came from non-Christian homes so we devised a program which the girls put on for their parents — as a means of evangelism. Then on Christmas Eve the faculty and students had a formal sit-down dinner together followed by a more informal program the next morning.

At the time my parents were living near Hiroshima, a 48-hour trip by a ferry and three trains from where I was teaching in Sapporo on the island of Hokkaido. To get home I would start on the afternoon of Christmas Eve and arrive home two days later where my parents and my older sister, Grace, were waiting for my arrival to celebrate Christmas. Most of Christmas Day I spent on the train by myself.

In spite of having such obstacles to overcome, I have many happy memories of the evangelistic emphasis in Christmas celebrations at the schools and churches I served in Japan. Also the Christmas spirit of love and joy I shared with my family still lives in my memory. Serving the Christ of Christmas in Japan was a great privilege. Now, in retirement, I still enjoy receiving many wonderful Christmas greetings and cards from Japanese Christian friends.

16

Harold Wilke

Christmas on Middle Eastern Sands

by Harold Wilke

Three camels plodded in a line on the sandy shore of the Mediterranean's sparkling blue water. A donkey brayed in the distance. Olive groves provided a dusty green background for a few small red-tile-roofed dwellings. Oranges and lemons hung from the trees in a citrus grove. A menorah carved from olive wood was just barely visible beside the entrance to one of the buildings. It was a perfect Christmas-card photo scene.

Surely this was no modern setting, but one 2,000 years old. Wasn't that the turf where Jesus of Nazareth played as a boy? Wasn't that menorah the very one carved by the carpenter Joseph? Weren't those villagers dressed in the Palestinian style one associated with Mary's garments? Surely I'd been transported in a time warp to the time when Jesus walked on earth.

But there *were* differences from those ancient days: Some people wandering about were obviously tourists from European ancestry. Then a car-horn broke the illusion and our own three boys paddled into sight, pushing an ungainly craft through the water for a ride on the waves. This was 1965 after all.

There was also a vast contrast between the children I was watching here play on the shore and those I'd been working with for six months in northern Germany. These children were playing with their hands while the ones I'd just left were from the thalidomide generation in Germany and England who tended to have disabilities such as the total loss of hands and arms so they had to learn to play using their toes instead of non-existent fingers.

Since I was born with no hands I'd been asked to show these several thousand children how I'd learned to cope with my birth defect. They were victims of a drug used by their mothers to overcome morning sickness in the second and third month of pregnancy which had unfortunately produced disastrous side effects, inhibiting the growth of parts of the body, resulting in many of them being born with severe disabilities.

After my stint of working with these children, their parents and care-givers as a consultant, our family was headed back to New York to arrive in time for the January school term via this two-week holiday in Tunisia and the south coast of the sun-drenched Mediterranean

Since we had finished up in Germany just before the Christmas holidays, we had enjoyed many Christmas festivities before we departed. Further, the Christmas theme had been tied in with the farewell ceremonies thanking me for the insights and new perspectives my ministry and expertise had given that generation of children in Germany, United Kingdom and Nordic lands, offering each of them new hope for a normal life.

So it seemed we had been granted two Christmases in one season! In spite of the bitter-sweet parting from Germany which had left us deeply imbued with concern for those children and their families, here we were in this seemingly ancient land celebrating Christmas all over again.

As I sat by the shores in that Holy Land watching my children at play, I was filled with faith and trust. After all this is the season when we celebrate hope for all — with special needs or not — rejoicing in the fantastic re-living of the Christmas experience and in the once-again-proclaimed assurance of God's grace to *all* humankind in the birth of Jesus.

17

Dick Smith (3rd from rt.)

The Old Miners' Christmas

by Richard Smith

"Here they come," my wife Bea exclaimed. "The first of the old miners is here!"

Leaning on a cane and carrying a burlap sack, Joe had walked from his flimsy, one-room shanty in Jere, West Virginia. Born in Czechoslovakia, he'd been here long enough to know that at the conclusion of the Christmas service there would be gifts of food — most welcome for these retired miners trying to eke out an existence on $18 a month.

Joe had been at "The Shack" for other reasons. As directors of this National Missions Presbyterian settlement house located in the heart of the coal mining district, we were prepared to be of service in time of need. Joe had been with us when we provided the primary refuge during three mine disasters. Though national media celebrated this community center for being a holistic, Christian service center, unsophisticated Joe simply had a warm spot in his heart for The Shack's caring ministry and had come during those difficult days to lend a hand.

Soon others trickled in to our Christmas party. Here was Mike, a disfigured Italian coal miner, who years before had been the victim of a coal mine roof cave-in. Sharp chunks of slate had scarred him permanently, but he still managed to hobble up the steps of The Shack.

Ivan, down from the steep West Virginia hill and across the railroad tracks — perhaps the oldest of our guests — like many who would join us for our Christmas celebration was foreign-born, a Russian. He needed help getting up the steps into The Shack's all-purpose room where the Christmas feast was spread. Mrs. Dodds, of the Women's Association of Morgantown's First Presbyterian Church, gave the aged miner a hand, helping Ivan to his seat at one of the long wooden tables beautifully decorated by various of the coal miners' wives.

A lovely Christmas tree in the corner of the room winked its welcome as recorded Christmas carols spoke of the coming of the Christ-child. On a platform up front, lighted candelabra reminded the miners of their Roman Catholic and Eastern Orthodox beginnings. A large picture of Christ testified to the underlying Christian unity of all. The visage of this pensive Christ seemed to embrace the disparity between the poorly-clothed, coal dust-touched, miners and the business-suited, distinguished guests. In Christ all are one and there was a basic equality in his presence.

The crowd included the owners of coal mines, the labor union executives and the president of the nearby public university. Then there was the ancient, Irish Catholic priest — Father Peter Finn who a half century ago considered Protestants a somewhat dubious lot.

Everyone was impressed with the superb holiday feast — turkey with dressing, cranberry sauce, pie and ice cream. They kept at it until no one could gobble any more — all the while served by happy volunteers in The Shack kitchen.

Following dessert, there were introductions and thank-yous, and then the Christmas story read from the Bible. Just before the benediction, there was a most memorable moment as the old miners began to sing "Silent Night, Holy Night" in more than a dozen languages. Some knew only one verse, others merely hummed, but their radiant faces truly glorified the Christ-child they had first known in so many distant lands.

Finally, as they left with Christmas cards and food parcels that would last for at least a month, the steps of these aged coal miners were visibly lighter, their eyes movingly brighter. We were glad to be part of the Christian community reaching out to those around us in the name of Christ who tells us all to bear one another's burdens for that is the will of God concerning us.

18

Ralph Galloway

A Christmas Dilemma in Zaire

by Ralph Galloway

Our youngest son Andrew was about to spend his last Christmas vacation with us in Kinshasa, Zaire before going off like the rest of our children to attend college in the United States. It was Christmas Eve, 1974, and I headed to the bank to withdraw some cash to do some last-minute shopping. We wanted this to be a memorable holiday and needed just a few more purchases for the Christmas feast.

Arriving at the bank I found the doors closed. Disappointed, I drove around the block to our church office. It too was closed. I asked a guard at the gate whom I recognized as one of the night watchmen why everything was closed down.

"Don't you know? Today has been declared a holiday."

I knew from previous years that usually Christmas Eve was only a half day of work so people could prepare for the evening services, but why the sudden change?

It appeared that Zaire's President Mobutu Sese Seco was to return that day from a visit to Communist China, and because he was wanting to curry favor with the Chinese hoping to get aid from them, he was declaring the day before Christmas to be a holiday while Christmas was to be a normal working day.

The population of Kinshasa was ordered to be at the airport to greet the president which meant the schools were closed so the school children could be transported to the airport. Secular holidays were the new order. Religious holidays were no longer to be holidays in Zaire.

This apparently was also meant as a power play against those Christian leaders who had criticized Mobutu's policies. There was a strong Christian presence in the country and traditionally church holy days had been national holidays even after the country gained its independence in 1960. Now some church leaders, hoping to curry favor, had made a public declaration that it didn't matter if December 25th was a holiday or not because scholars had never agreed on the date Jesus was born in Bethlehem. Besides the Greek Orthodox celebrate Christmas on a different date.

As Pastor of the French International Parish of Kinshasa, I had scheduled the usual Christmas Eve service for the French parish. That afternoon at the church I met with the members of the choir who were all highly indignant at the preemptory action and they said, "We are going to sing and praise God all night even if we have to go to work tomorrow. It is better to go to work feeling tired just to show that we think Christmas is more important to us than the president."

And so the preparations went forward. The choir was practicing, others were weaving palm branches into braided wreaths with bright red hibiscus flowers interspersed throughout. These in turn were being tied to the pillars that held up the roof and to the arch over the entrance of the vestibule.

The service that evening was packed. Besides our regular choir, there were several visiting choral groups. The service consisted of a lot of singing, readings from scripture and dramatic presentations by various Sunday school classes depicting the birth of Jesus. This celebration went on till dawn of Christmas Day.

Similar services were held in churches throughout Zaire. In one parish where a church leader present rose to explain why Christmas could no longer be a holiday, a woman parishioner got up and roundly denounced him for claiming Christmas was no longer a church holiday. "Do you mean to tell us after all these years of celebrating the incarnation of God on the 25th of December, it no longer matters anymore? You should be ashamed for giving in to unbelievers!"

Obviously the church authorities, in trying to get in good with the government, had lost face in the eyes of the Christians they were supposed to lead. Soon a strongly worded church pronouncement was published proclaiming Christmas as the day traditionally set aside for remembering our Savior's birth and reminding Christians to remember God's grace with festive celebrations on that day.

Christmas of 1974 remains in my mind the Christmas when

the women in the church stood up to the male leadership and pointed them in the right direction. It surprised no one when the following week the church leaders publicly rescinded their stance on Christmas, acknowledging that this was the day we agree to celebrate our Lord's birth and his coming to earth to reconcile us all to our Creator.

I was gratified that at least the Christian women in Zaire kept their theology straight and didn't hesitate calling the church leaders to repentance.

19

Betty and Frank Newman

Our Best Christmas Ever

by Betty Newman

It was 1942 and China was at war. We had come back to the States as a family so we were safely away from the hostilities, but then Frank was asked by the mission board to return to China, if need be alone. We applied for visas, but the Chinese government refused to grant any women or children permission to travel in that war-torn land. Thus Frank set out alone, traveling across the Pacific by ship along with 7,000 American troops headed for North Africa.

The ship was called the *Mauritania* but I was sworn to secrecy and so could not disclose its name or its destination to anyone. Suddenly the terrifying word came that the Japanese were claiming to have sunk the *Mauritania*. Our government made no public comments on the report, so I was left to fret. Then to my great joy and thanksgiving, three months later just as Christmas was approaching there came a cable informing us that Frank was safe in Hunan.

That was our first momentous Christmas gift.

Many families were separated throughout the war and ours was no exception. Two years went by rather quickly. Like other women during those days I had to fill in as both mother and father and keep our family pasted together while coping with wartime privations and shortages. Finally word came that Frank was shortly going to be on his way back to the States. No date had been set and with war-time restrictions we would not be informed on which ship he would travel.

Christmas 1944 drew near. We all seemed to be living disrupted lives. Sherman Skinner, a dear friend who lived in Philadelphia, had recently lost his wife leaving him alone to raise their two boys. He knew the holidays would be a difficult time and so he phoned us in Ventnor, New Jersey to invite me and my three children to come for a Christmas visit. His brother was going to join us, so Sherman promised we could share our joys and loneliness together.

Since our children were all good friends and close in age, they were enthusiastic about the idea. I gratefully accepted the invitation knowing that it would be fun for the children to have playmates, but also appreciative of the fact that Sherman not only had a big house with plenty of room, but he had an excellent cook and housekeeper.

We left the Jersey shore and wended our way to Philadelphia by train. Sherman met us in the midst of frightfully cold weather replete with snow and ice. The children would have to do most of their playing indoors if the weather didn't turn nicer.

Shortly after arriving in Philadelphia, word was forwarded to us that Frank was finally on his way back to the States. Still no date was given when we could expect him, so we all banded together to pray for his safe homecoming.

The wait became burdensome as I tried not to think about what was happening to Frank on his long journey back to us. Our dinner the second night was interrupted when Sherman got a phone call. He went to the study to answer it and soon I heard him shout my name, "Betty!"

I ran into the study where Sherman informed me, "We have to pick up an important gift someone wants to give us. I need you to go with me."

"Not I, Sherman," I protested, "we can't go off and leave our children in this awful weather. I'm sure the gift can wait until later."

Sherman looked so hurt I began to relent.

"Believe me, Betty," he persisted, "we have to go now. The weather isn't that bad and besides Sadie will watch the children while we're gone. It should not take long."

Against my better judgment I gave in, reluctantly. In spite of the inclement weather, Sherman seemed to be traveling too fast down the main thoroughfare, so I protested, "Drive carefully, Sherman, think of the children!"

My warning didn't seem to slow him down at all and I was beginning to get irritated at his recklessness. But just then we approached a small nearby railway station and to my amazement I realized that was my own darling Frank standing out in the middle of the road, in the snow, waiting to surprise me.

Sherman had barely come to a halt when I leapt from the car into Frank's outstretched arms.

The rest of the story is short. We were oblivious to the snow and the road until Sherman came barreling out of the car shouting at us, "If you two don't get out of the middle of the road there will be no Christmas for anybody!"

We returned to our senses, climbed into the car and then drove home again to assure our children that our prayers had been answered. Their father was safely home from China and our family was to be united for the holidays.

Next to the gift of the Bethlehem Babe, God had given us the most wonderful gift of all. It was our greatest Christmas ever!

20

Marcia Ball

Christmas Caroling in Zimbabwe

by Marcia Mary Ball

Going Christmas caroling is usually a fun adventure whether it is snowing and six degrees below zero, or at the Church of the Nativity in Bethlehem where pilgrims travel from afar to commemorate Christ's birth, or in hospital corridors where the lilting voices help patients forget their ills.

But for those born in the northern hemisphere, it is difficult to adjust to Christmas south of the equator where Christmas falls in the middle of summer. Usually the heat makes you so limp, happy spirits are hard to develop. Thus it surprised everyone one hot summer night when we decided to import our northern caroling custom to Zimbabwe, Africa.

They say that nightfall is the "winter" of the tropics, so perhaps it was the heat that addled us sufficiently that when night came someone suggested we missionaries should go caroling to demonstrate to the rest of the folk on the mission station what it entailed. We were 80 miles out in the bush on a remote mission station.

Off we set — a doctor, two nurses, a dentist and three school teachers. The only others on the mission station — who had never heard of such a custom — were the African school teachers, nurses and the doctor plus the minister and a few maintenance people, all snug in their homes that evening.

Accompanying the revelers were Buffie, a lovable golden retriever; Katie, a saucy wirehaired terrier; Wolfie, an affectionate curly-haired Schnauzer; and Dickie, a small French poodle. The pets all knew each other and thought it was a great romp as we walked along. Fortunately they kept their voices down when we stopped to sing.

Our surprised African friends and their families crowded to the doors and windows to see what the commotion was about as we stopped at each house. After each song they happily applauded our yuletide efforts and then asked what it was all about. When we explained, the listeners got their hymn books and joined us as we headed toward the next house.

The group had grown to over 30 by the time we reached the last house — our minister's home. The singing brought him to the door and after we explained the custom, he approved warmly, then closed our excursion with an appropriate prayer.

As we separated children, dogs and people, a beautiful shooting star arched across the heavens putting a grand finale on our efforts. With shouts of "Merry Christmas" we turned homeward filled with the joy of which we had been singing.

21

Lillian and Larry Driskill

A Grand Japanese Christmas Party

by J. Lawrence Driskill

We were rather surprised to find ourselves serving hot cocoa and peanut butter cookies to 150 Japanese junior high students and their parents one Christmas Eve in 1953. We had
casually invited the students from our Christian school, Seikyo
Gakuen, to drop by at the end of a joyful night of Christmas
caroling around the neighborhood in our small town of Kawa-
chinagano, near Osaka. A lot more guests than we had expected
showed up — they probably wanted to taste American goodies

combined with a curiosity to see our new missionary home.

It had been a busy time for me — I had already helped conduct a dozen special Christmas services in the churches, schools and homes of our area. Our pastor, Toru Hashimoto, had stressed that Christmas was a wonderful time to win new people to Christ because the Japanese were naturally curious about Christmas celebrations — and so would listen to stories about the Christ-child. The Christmas caroling by our students was the crowning touch as they wended their way to homes where caroling would be welcomed, concentrating on those where shut-ins would be cheered with Christmas light and joy.

But about three times as many had turned out to carol as had been expected. Thus when the caroling ended we were faced with the challenge of getting 150 celebrators into our home for the closing worship service and refreshments. Expecting some 50 people, we thought we had more than enough. We had bought 50 cups and stockpiled enough cocoa, powdered milk and sugar to serve alongside the cookies Lillian and a helper had baked. When we learned how many had showed up for the caroling, some quick changes had to be made.

Fortunately stores were still open so Lillian got some extra supplies and then scrounged all the empty cups she could from our neighbors. Fortunately some of the students stepped in to help out and in the end there was plenty for everyone.

It also helped that since the young people were caroling in separate groups, not all of them arrived at the same time. One of the first young girls to arrive slipped out of her shoes in the spacious entrance way and said, "Although your house is in Western style, it is like our Japanese homes in some ways. For example, you have a big entrance way where we can take off our shoes. And you don't crowd the rooms with furniture."

"Thank you," I replied, explaining, "Usually we do have more furniture than you see now. To make room for this large meeting tonight, we moved our dining room table and some other pieces to our garage. As you can see, our Japanese-style sliding doors have been opened so the dining room and living room form one huge meeting room."

Although the young teenagers laughed, joked and jostled each other, they were amazingly well-behaved all evening. By setting up a cafeteria-style assembly line from the front hall, through the kitchen and on through the dining and living rooms we managed to organize and feed everyone. Those who finished their refreshments first graciously returned their dishes to the kitchen for washing and recycling.

It was standing room only for the closing worship service with students listening through open doors from every nearby room. Finally some left and we managed to have a few fun games and songs when the crowd thinned down to about the original 50 we had expected. Around midnight the last stragglers departed leaving us with nothing but joyful memories of a glorious Christmas celebration. We had been too occupied even to think about being homesick for our loved ones from whom we were separated this Christmas.

Best of all, the Christian seeds sown among those students later reaped a good harvest. Several dedicated their lives and their professions to serving the Christ whose birth we celebrated that Christmas.

22

Clara Lindholm

A Surprise Christmas Gift

by **Clara Lindholm**

The Christmas of 1915 was fast approaching. I was ten, my brother eight. Our world was filled with enormous white sparkling snowdrifts, the happy jingle of sleigh bells and people going and coming encased in mufflers, muffs, mittens and heavy coats.

This was Minnesota where winters are crisp and cold. Even as schoolmates and neighbors exchanged cheery greetings, we tried to hide our heavy and sad hearts. Our father had recently died and since he had left no will, the prolonged probate-court proceedings had deprived Mother of adequate financial funds. We knew this Christmas she could not afford to give us the toys and gifts we had come to expect in the past.

One day there appeared in the window of the village grocery store a large glass jar filled with bright colored marbles. Beside it stood a new sled, trimmed in red and with gleaming, polished runners. Long and low — it was called a coaster. Underneath the jar was a sign which said, "GUESS THE CORRECT NUMBER OF MARBLES AND THE SLED IS YOURS. DRAWING ON CHRISTMAS EVE AT 4 P.M."

"Wouldn't it be wonderful if we could win that prize?" my brother asked.

"Yes," I replied, "but wouldn't Mother be better able to guess a more correct number than we? Let's go ask her."

Mother saw the eagerness in our eyes as we described the sled and asked her to try to win it. Day after day she studied that jar, counting as best she could the top layer and then estimating how many layers there were.

Knowing that many people would be participating in the contest, Mother warned us, "We have to realize that we may not win. Let's determine to be happy for whoever it is who wins. I will try my best but so will others. We must remember that we already have Jesus as the wonderful Christmas gift God has given us."

At last she had decided upon a number, wrote it on a slip of paper, signed it and placed it in the box provided. The days passed all too slowly. Finally Christmas Eve arrived and finally it was time for the drawing. Many eager parents and children gathered at the store.

The store owner welcomed us, made a short speech and said, "The number of marbles in the jar is 876." Someone wrote the number plainly on the blackboard as the owner continued, "Now I will draw from the box all the numbers submitted. The person coming closest to the right number will be the winner. Numbers will be recorded on the blackboard in columns by hundreds — 300 to 400, 400 to 500 in another, etc."

The slips from the box were withdrawn one by one and recorded. Finally the last slip was drawn. People held their breath in anticipation. The store owner scanned all the numbers in the 800 column and in a few minutes called out, "869 is the winner. The slip is signed by Sadie Malbon. Will you please come forward, Mrs. Malbon, to accept your prize."

Mother's eyes filled with tears but a smile of gratitude brightened her face. She accepted the sled while the crowd clapped for her victory. They seemed to know she now had a Christmas gift for her children. Though shared with my brother, that beautiful bright and shiny sled is the only Christmas gift I remember from my childhood.

Later, in gratitude for God's Christmas gift of Jesus, I went to the mission field in China and the Philippines, because I wanted to tell others about God's wonderful Christmas gift to the world. There, by God's grace, I was able to serve our Lord for 39 years.

23

Dorothy Parker

My First Christmas in India

by Dorothy Parker

I didn't know what to expect my first Christmas in India, but I knew the holiday would be different in this distinct culture. When we received an invitation to see a Christmas play at a not too distant village, I brightened. I knew how the people of India loved drama, so this should be fun.

It was dark when we started out, the sky bright with stars.

We laughed and joked as the car jolted over the rough set of ruts that passed for a road. By request we brought two Petromax lights — similar to Coleman lamps — to serve as the play's footlights. Also we brought small bags of peanuts and sesame seed hard candy to be handed out afterwards.

When we arrived we hung the lights from nearby trees and then were shown our seats. As "guests" — and foreigners — we had iron chairs. Our reputations preceded us, for our friends knew how difficult it was for us to sit too long cross-legged.

All proper plays in India are preceded by a period of singing. We heard a mix of English tunes with Hindi words plus Indian tunes, the *bhajans*, expressing joy in the season. The pastor then blessed the occasion with a lengthy prayer. Finally it was time for the play to begin.

The tableau was complete. On a crudely put together stage with no curtains nor lighting aside from our Petromax lights — plus the moon shining brightly above the eastern horizon — there soon appeared the shepherds leading five goats and a kid. They gazed with proper awe on Mary riding an ass led by Joseph, plus a real baby who blessedly slept throughout the performance. After a proper reading the Magi arrived replete with camel (borrowed from a nearby village where a man had one for hire). Their speeches were interspersed with more songs appropriate to the story. Finally the villains — Herod's men come to slaughter the children — were foiled and Mary rode off on the ass, singing a lullaby. The holy family was safe.

At the end of this wonderful presentation, it seemed almost sacrilegious to distribute bags of peanuts and candy. We were a hushed group heading back home, awestruck anew at the never tiresome story of the First Christmas. We too had heard the angels tell their glad tidings.

24

Eleanor and Bob Lazear

Christmas in Colombia

by Robert Lazear

Christmas holidays in Colombia actually begin in November with the end of the school year, so Christmas and the New Year come in the middle of summer vacation. Not too many Christmas carols are to be heard since Christmas is more commonly celebrated with fireworks. All kinds of explosives are legal so the sky lights up on Christmas and New Year's Day till nearly dawn with a constant bang-pop-hiss-roar-thud that all but drowns out conversation.

Because of parental persuasion and guidance, our children did little with fireworks, but they thoroughly enjoyed another Colombian custom — sending tissue-paper hot-air balloons high into the night sky. They made these by gluing strips of brightly colored tissue paper in happy designs over thin globe-shaped frames. A wire ring placed in the opening at the bottom held cotton or cloth impregnated with kerosene. When this wick was ignited, the flames lit the balloon and soon the hot air lofted it on high.

It was quite a sight to see these colorful globes float high in the night sky. An added adventure was to chase the globes as they came down trying to save them from crashing in order to send them up again. Since Colombia has so much rainfall, the possibility of these sinking balloons causing fires was nominal.

For most people in Colombia, Christmas is a time for family reunions with special meals, usually roast turkey and the trimmings, but no mince or pumpkin pie. Instead *buñuelos* (a kind of doughnut without a hole) and *natilla* (a creamy topping) were the desserts everyone looked forward to. An *arbolito* or "little tree" which probably is not an evergreen is set up and decorated before Christmas. Often this will be just a bare branch on which they dangle ornaments.

Of course the stores tend to display pictures of traditional Christmas scenes from Merrie Olde England complete with snow. (This is about the only place you'll see snow depicted in Colombia. Since it is so near the equator and the climate is so tropical all year no one ever thinks of snow. Although it is cooler in the mountains, it never snows except for on a few remote, uninhabited peaks people tend to forget are there.)

It is much more traditional in Colombia to have a manger scene or creche in their homes and churches. Some of these are most elaborate. Many families add a figure to the creche each day for the nine days before Christmas. Finally on Christmas Eve the Baby Jesus is placed in the manger. The tradition of daily devotions during the nine days before Christmas (known as a *novena*) was originally Catholic, but many Protestant churches also observe it.

Colombian tradition has the Baby Jesus (*el Nino Dios* — the God Child) appear on Christmas Eve leaving presents at the foot of the bed and some children write to tell him what they want. In some families presents are exchanged on January 6 (Epiphany) when the Three Kings make their visit, but most Colombians do not exchange gifts. Often there is no money; every peso is needed for food and shelter.

For most Colombians, it's enough to celebrate the Yuletide season by getting together for holiday meals. Commercial interests are trying to promote gift-giving. Decorations and television commercials show Santa Claus more and more often (*Papá Noel* in Spanish) but so far the idea is obviously imported and has little impact. No child would think of writing to *Papá Noel*.

Christmas is celebrated on December 24th. Catholics go to midnight mass while Protestants usually have an earlier church service in which children participate in a Christmas pageant. Sometimes the drama is rather lifelike as Mary and Joseph escape from Herod on a live donkey down the center aisle of the church. I've seen slight liberties taken with the story as Herod chasing after them takes out his frustration on the people in the front pews who let them escape! This is followed by a time of singing *villancicos* or carols, followed by a time of fellowship and candy for the children.

On December 28 Herod's massacre of the innocents is commemorated with the Colombian equivalent of our April Fool's Day — a time for practical jokes. Best be wary if someone claims there's a bug crawling up your back. Even newspapers will publish startling reports which aren't true at all. A disclaimer elsewhere will remind the reader it's an *inocentada*.

New Year's Eve tends to find many churchgoers in a *vigilia* or all-night worship service followed by a fellowship meal for everyone. Then come the games and the traditional New Year customs like eating twelve grapes at midnight, as a wish is made for each month of the year.

Most of all, as my colleague Alice Winters who taught in the seminary in Barranquilla reminded us in a recent Christmas letter, "Christmas in Colombia is a season of laughter, love, and joy because of Jesus Christ. Misery and suffering are not forgotten, but strength is renewed for the year to come."

25

Christy and Betty Wilson

Christmas in Afghanistan

by J. Christy Wilson, Jr.

Since Christmas is not widely celebrated in Afghanistan, a Muslim country, for Christians there is even greater reason to honor Jesus' birthday. It is also a wonderful opportunity in a land where he is not known to explain to friends and neighbors why we commemorate Christ's coming to earth.

While we lived in that country, the Kabul Community Christian Church made it a practice to present a beautiful Christmas pageant for three evenings preceding Christmas. This dramatic presentation was done in the large garden of the church, and for those nights several hundred Afghan people and members of the foreign community would come to watch this production. Since winters can be very cold in Kabal, everyone would come to this outdoor presentation well wrapped in warm clothes.

The Christmas story with beautiful Christmas music was all recorded on tape, so those in the play — Mary, Joseph, the shepherds, the angels, the Magi and King Herod — did not have to worry about learning parts but could concentrate on their acting as the tape progressed, Mary riding in on a white donkey and Joseph were annually rebuffed at the inn door and shown to the stable with cows and sheep standing by. The farm animals came from nearby farmers, while the camels were "rented" from a local camel caravan whose owners brought them and led them through their paces.

One night a lamb fell into a well left uncovered. This caused a lot of confusion until the frantic animal was rescued and the performance could begin. The camels were the huge hybrid Bactrian kind and it was always a thrill to hear the marshal music announcing their arrival with the three richly dressed Magi. Watching their shadows play across the tall elm trees bordering the garden made it seem all the more realistic.

The angels were a problem. How could they be made to appear suddenly? Finally the dilemma was resolved by having them stand on a high platform behind a black cloth. At the first notes of "Hark the Herald Angels Sing" the cloth was dropped and suddenly the angels appeared, as if from the sky, in all their glory.

What a great joy it was to share this marvelous message with the dear Afghan people: "Today in the town of David a Savior has been born to you. He is Christ the Lord."

26

Mary Ruth and Harold Hanlin

A Wartime Christmas

by Harold Hanlin

Christmas 1945 I found myself stationed on the Marshallese island of Kwajalein as a chaplain for American military forces. I had been invited to hold Sunday services on the nearby island of Carlos two days before Christmas when a Marshallese friend, Daniel, informed me that he not only wanted to accompany me to Carlos that Sunday, but that the people on the island also wanted me to return for a Christmas celebration the following Tuesday. When I seemed perplexed why they would want me to return so soon after the Sunday service, Daniel explained that the people on Carlos wanted to show their appreciation for the Americans saving them from enemy occupation.

It didn't make much sense to me, but Daniel patiently explained that the Sunday service was for a communion service, while the Tuesday gathering was for a Christmas celebration. Then he explained we should be ready to leave at seven on Tuesday morning. It was finally decided that Mr. Waterman, the new Red Cross field director, two Navy officers, several enlisted men and two other Marshallese men, Anjerok and Henry, would all be part of the expedition. Sadly when the morning came Daniel was sick and couldn't go.

The group consulted about what gifts to take along to give to the local children. Mr. Waterman found a case of hard candy and I arranged several cases of chewing gum from a friend. So on Christmas morning we set off, making short shift of the ten-mile sea journey to Carlos in a Navy blunt-nosed landing craft called a LCVP.

Once there we were met by Pastor Langrin, the minister of the Carlos church, plus a few members of the church who escorted us to a long building which had once served as barracks for enemy soldiers. Now several local families left homeless by the war were using the abandoned building as living quarters. Some were barely out of bed by the time we arrived — which embarrassed them because they were not ready to begin the promised Christmas program.

Half the building had been converted into a meeting hall. We were escorted there and invited to sit on the few folding chairs extant. The rest would sit on the floor, apparently.

Finally the program got under way with a traditional worship service led by Pastor Langrin in Marshallese. We couldn't understand the words, but the congregation enthusiastically nodded approval and said "Amen" in appropriate places. At Pastor Langrin's request, I gave the closing prayer.

When the service was over Pastor Langrin invited the children to come in. Suddenly some 60 children began marching in with the smallest in front. They sat down on the floor in an orderly fashion. Amazingly the children had memorized four hymns in English and sang them perfectly. Then came two songs in Marshallese, beautifully harmonized, with no musical accompaniment. Mrs. Elsie Liokwor, whose husband had been killed in an enemy bombing raid, was their able leader. As they sang she walked back and forth beating time for them with her hands, giving them instruction or encouragement as needed.

The children were then handed Christian pennants made of stiff paper with a red cross drawn on them which they waved in time to the music during some of the songs and dances. Another stage prop intrigued me — a large curtain background with trees, Christmas symbols and even a Navy symbol like the one I wore on my uniform, but everything was strangely upside down! I wondered if it was a mistake.

Many of the children were wearing or carrying bracelets, necklaces and headbands, and others carried similar things in their hands. At one point they began going around the room, saying "Merry Christmas" and then repeating a Bible verse while putting a necklace or bracelet on each of us. Some of these had been made of beautiful seashells which the children had diligently searched out on nearby beaches.

Soon everyone joined the throng of marchers, going around the room giving one another such things as boxes of matches, bars of soap and small items bought at the Navy commissary. The Christmas spirit of love and joy abounded. I was touched especially by an old lady who could not march fast enough to keep up with the others. She took the hand of a little girl who couldn't walk fast either and the two of them conducted their own march of love around the room.

Finally the Christmas program came to a close. It was then the background curtain I was worried about was quickly turned into an upright position so the pictures and symbols were in the proper position again. Finally it became clear this was a profound statement: "Although enemy occupation turned our whole world upside down, you Americans have put our world in its right position again. Thank you!"

This was articulated in the closing statement when one of the elders stepped forward and with a cord began lowering a large star from near the ceiling. On it was written, "Thank you missionaries and American military people. You have brought great blessings to this island. Thanks be to God and to you as God's messengers for setting things right for us again. Through you, God has brought us from darkness to light."

It was a wonderful closure to a lovely program. I returned to Kwajalein and shared this wonderful Christmas experience with my sick friend Daniel. Then I sent a letter describing it all to Mary Ruth back in America so that she and the children could participate a bit in my life across all the miles that separated us during this Christmas at the end of that tragic World War II.

27

Alma and Fred Schneider and family

An Only Bed in Brazil at Christmas

by Fred Schneider

During the Christmas holiday season in 1948 I was visiting congregations in Brazil. Every day I found myself scheduled to be in a different locale, so I found myself passed on from one Christian family to the next. One evening after a service in a rural area some 20 miles outside the town of Santa Rosa in the state of Rio Grande do Sul, I received several invitations from various ones in the church to go home with them for the night. One elderly couple, well along in years and rather feeble, strongly insisted I be their guest, so I acquiesced. It was evident they were respected by other members of the congregation who reluctantly granted them their wish.

Someone had brought them to the service in their horse-drawn wagon. Now I joined them for their return trip home to their small house close to a creek, not far from the main dirt road. The house had two rooms — one serving as a combination kitchen and living room, the other a bedroom. The bedroom had a Dutch door with an upper and lower part. After a wonderful evening of fellowship discussing the Christian life, Scriptures and general experiences, it was time to retire for the night so we stopped for prayer.

After we had all prayed, the couple lit a lamp and led me into the bedroom to show me where I was to sleep. There was only one bed with a corn-husk mattress. They said if I needed to get up during the night there was a small outhouse near the creek, but I should be careful because there were some large snakes around. They then returned to the kitchen.

Though tired and weary, I found it difficult to go to sleep because I kept wondering where they were going to sleep, since I was in their only bed. During that restless night I finally decided to get up and go outside. As I quietly opened the top portion of the bedroom's door I stood in utter amazement. A full moon shining through the kitchen window showed the couple in front of the kitchen stove. The husband was curled up on a sheep pelt at the feet of his dear wife who was sitting in a rocker with a little blanket over her lap.

Quietly I made my way out and in again without waking them, but never shall I forget the sight of that sweet elderly Christian couple in front of that stove. They had only one bed, yet they insisted on inviting me to spend the night regardless of their own discomfort. The Babe of Bethlehem did not appear to them that year, but they knew that by welcoming the "least" of them, they were welcoming the Lord.

28

Kirby and Hal Davis

My Favorite Christmas Memory

by **Kirby Filson Davis**

On Christmas Sunday, 1982, my mother took the entire congregation out to dinner. People were already wearing "I survived the Blizzard of '82" tee shirts. The roads were still almost impassable following a Christmas Eve snowstorm that brought Denver to a complete stop.

If anything could demonstrate that weathermen are fallible, it was this storm. They had predicted a little snow — not unheard of in Colorado, but the storm actually dumped and dumped snow over the city until drifts piled so high doors wouldn't open and garages became prisons for the cars that couldn't drive through the waist-high snow anyway.

My husband Hal, pastor of Trinity Presbyterian Church, was of the strong opinion that Sunday services should never be canceled, even if he were the only intrepid slogger to make it to church. But four hardy souls managed to show up — a girl who could play a few hymns, another willing to sing a solo and a couple who drove a four-wheel-drive vehicle.

My mother, then 85, and I had decided to stay home, when the phone rang. The couple with the four-wheel-drive were willing to come get us if we were brave enough to venture out. My mother, Wilma Filson, ever a hardy soul, leapt at the chance, so out we ventured. The car skid hardly at all, and suddenly the sun came out making the snow sparkle.

But the service was warm and we were glad we'd come. A special fellowship bound our hardly little group together and to celebrate the joy of that Christmas season, Mother Wilma took the entire congregation out to dinner!

Editor's Note: Wilma Filson, now 98, still practices that wonderful spirit of love and joy she demonstrated the year of the Christmas blizzard. We know this firsthand for she has been our neighbor across the street for over a decade. Often we reminisce together about her years at McCormick Seminary in Chicago where her husband, Dr. Floyd Filson, was a much-beloved professor.

29

Betty Hessel

Christmas at Pala Pala

by **Elizabeth A. Hessel**

One of my missionary assignments in the Philippines was serving as the registrar of the Union Theological Seminary. The school had prospered and grown so, we decided to move to larger quarters. A fine plot of undeveloped land area between the two barrios of Bukal and Pala Pala was chosen for the site.

Only after we moved did we discover that for years the people of these two Philippine barrios had a deep-seated vendetta going between them. No one could even tell us the cause of the feud—it had gone on so long, everyone seemed to have forgotten the cause of the enmity. We just knew this deep, often violent, distrust of each other had to stop.

As part of the seminary's outreach program, we started inviting our neighbors to our church services. At first only a few people straggled in, but gradually the congregation grew. A small chapel was built and soon we had a youth program made up of young people from both communities.

As Christmas approached, the young people informed me they wanted to prepare the Christmas evening program with no help from their elders. "Oh, well," they added, "you can get the wood for an outdoor stage, help us get lights, and also you can supply the costumes. But nothing else!"

So it went. On the one hand I was pleased the young people wanted to go it alone, but on the other hand I was a bit nervous about what they could pull off and wished I could help guide the production.

A rickety stage was constructed, electric bulbs connected to a generator were strung, and some 80 chairs were moved out of the chapel. Excitement was running high among the young people. I was wondering whether the older generation from both Pala Pala and Bukal would come. Each contingency would have to walk the dark highway, a kilometer each way. This road had witnessed many hold-ups and even a recent murder. Would someone start a fight and ruin our Christmas program?

The night for the Christmas program arrived. A small moon was high in the sky bright with stars. A soft, tropical evening welcomed the crowd. Soon the chairs filled up leaving many others standing, all mesmerized by the program.

Christmas carols were followed by a portrayal of the Bible

story. The holy family came on stage creating a serene tableau. Then came the shepherds, one carrying a live baby kid — but none too firmly. Suddenly the scared young goat broke loose, jumped off the stage with actors and some audience participants running in hot pursuit. Eventually order was restored and the scenes continued.

Herod entered with crown and robe. In talking with the three Magi, Herod's crown (which I had made) managed to tumble off, making the audience laugh. "Herod" so enjoyed this crowd-pleasing technique, he managed to have his crown fall off two more times. The comedy relieved my tension and the fear I had of a fight breaking out between these two factions. Then it dawned on me that this was probably the first time many of the audience had heard the Christmas story. I was miserable thinking what an impression this fiasco was making. Finally the program came to a close with everyone singing "Silent Night."

I felt some comfort in the beauty of that beloved hymn. As we stood to leave I began to realize that the barrio people were speaking to one another, wishing each other *Maligayang Pasko Po* (Merry Christmas). Then everyone headed home, some north, some south.

When I explained to one of my fellow missionaries my distress that such an opportunity to tell the Christmas story had been so badly botched, I was told emphatically: "This has been a wonderfully blessed night. Just think! the residents of both Pala Pala and Bukal came together on this beautiful night greeting one another in peace and singing 'Silent Night.' What more could you hope for?"

I stopped worrying and was thankful that this Christmas spirit of love and joy had helped to begin the healing between these two warring barrios.

30

Florence Antablin

The Cross at Christmas in Arab Lands

by Florence Antablin

For centuries the cross has been an important Christian
symbol, for Christians believe our savior came to earth to die
to save the world. Thus the cross and Christmas are irrevocably
linked for Christians. Unfortunately Muslims in Saudi Arabia
are deeply offended by any connection made between the birth
of Jesus and the cross.

To Muslims, the cross is an enigma. Though they believe that Jesus was a great prophet, they find it impossible to believe God would allow Jesus to die in such a shameful manner. Beyond this, since the cross is seen universally as a symbol of the Christian faith, Muslims not only do not understand it, they are offended by it. To accommodate these sensibilities, when American military chaplains arrive in Saudi Arabia on temporary duty, the U.S. embassy personnel ask them to remove even the crosses from the lapels of their uniforms before disembarking from the aircraft.

Crosses, however, keep turning up in Saudi Arabia. They of course appear in building construction, since most structures are built with vertical and horizontal supports — the essential elements of a cross. Even a prominent minaret in the capital city of Riyadh was found to have perfect crosses inadvertently built into the structure on all sides of its slender minaret. Soon after this beautiful minaret was completed, it was redesigned in order to eliminate the crosses altogether.

Then someone spotted a cross on the new logo of the Saudi Airlines. Apparently in the word "Saudi" negative space was created between the lower-case letters "s" and "a" so that as they face each other, the space between them formed a perfect cross. This logo was changed at enormous cost to eliminate this appearance on everything from tickets to airplanes.

One Christmas when I was in Riyadh — 1992 — the Christian community gathered, as usual to have their yuletide celebration. A facility far out of the city was chosen for the event because it was large enough to hold the numerous Christians from all over the world who were employed by the Saudi government. The gathering was especially blessed by the unexpected appearance of a cross.

Finding Christmas decorations was almost impossible, not to mention illegal, but someone with Scandinavian connections managed to import a shipment of fresh evergreens. When they arrived they were brought out to decorate the hall for the Christmas celebration. In the barren desert wastes of the interior of Arabia that, in itself, was a miracle.

Since tree decorations were not available, it was decided to bank these lovely greens on the platform in an artistic fashion to create a winterland backdrop. This done, we stepped back to see how the evergreens looked. Suddenly we realized that without anyone trying to create such an effect, there at the center of the arrangement, standing tall and upright against the pulpit was a large evergreen branch forming a beautiful cross with its two horizontal branches extending out on each side of the central stem.

We were all awed by the realization that even natural things were giving witness to the precious symbol of our faith in that land where the cross is prohibited and not to be seen. We left our Christmas celebration convinced that no earthly power can permanently exclude the Christ of Christmas or his saving cross. Christmas and the cross will always remain connected, even in those lands that are hostile to the cross.

Bethlehem's Gift

by James B. Douthitt

Rome gave to the world her armed might
Athens her culture, clear and bright
But lowly Bethlehem on the plain
Gave us a Savior, bless his name.

Crete gave the world her ships untold
Jerusalem her temple's gold
But Bethlehem — best gift of all
Jesus, by whom we rise or fall.

Of all the cities of the world
Or all the flags that e'er were furled
The greatest gift that any gave
Was Christ who came, the world to save.

Part II

Christmas Traditions Around the World

1

Origins of Christmas, Gift Giving, Pageants and Christmas Music

At Christmas time millions of people around our globe in myriad tongues sing "Joy to the world! ... let earth receive her King." The glorious birth of our Lord, Jesus Christ, is the real "reason for the season," but the Early Church was late in finding an official date for this joyful event. The December 25th date was eventually set in the fifth century, but no one knew the exact date of our Lord's birth.

Earlier in 336 Emperor Constantine I had chosen December 25th as the date for the Mithraic rites of the "birth of the sun" and the close of the Saturnalia festival. If any popular secular festival could be considered "appropriate" for becoming the date for Christmas, this was it. Romans believed the Saturnalia festival commemorated that happy period under the Roman divinity Saturn when freedom and equality reigned and violence and oppression were unknown. During this festival business affairs ceased, masters and slaves changed places and gifts were exchanged. Sadly it had one great weakness that also carried over for some revelers at Christmas time — excessive indulgence and license.

The name "Christmas" came from the Medieval English "Christes Masse" (the Mass of Christ). That name is now known all over the world. For us today the real origin for gift giving at Christmas is based on God's gift of Christ, "God so loved that he gave his only Son" (Jn 3:16). The Bible tells us that the Magi also gave gifts to the Baby Jesus. Where Christians can afford to do so, Christmas gift giving is widely practiced.

For many years now Christmas pageants have been another important element of Christmas celebrations. For this we owe thanks to St. Francis of Assisi who began this tradition the Christmas of 1224 in the Italian town of Greccio. There St. Francis constructed a manger, tying to it a donkey and an ox. He then gathered clergy friends and other believers together to pray at the manger. One retired soldier claimed he "saw" the Baby Jesus in the manger. This started the tradition of putting a baby in the manger — either a live one or a doll.

Since then the manger scene or "creche" has become popular in many lands. Eventually it became customary to put small figures around the manger to represent the Holy Family, the shepherds, the Magi, angels as well as animals such as donkeys, sheep, camels and oxen. Usually a star is also placed above the manger scene. Recreating this scene "live" is the essence of the Christmas drama or pageant — living out the events of the first Christmas at Bethlehem.

German and Alpine artisans began to carve figures of Joseph, Mary and the Baby Jesus from native woods. Soon these artistic figures were placed in homes, churches and even in marketplaces. When Moravians emigrated to America in the 18th century they brought with them some of these nativity figures. Their first permanent settlement in America was called "Bethlehem". The name was chosen on Christmas Eve, 1741, during their first Christmas worship service in the New World. Thus Bethlehem, Pennsylvania was named.

The Moravians called the manger scene a "*Putz*" (from the German "to decorate"). Beginning with their *Putz* in Bethlehem, this Moravian Community Putz became a model for many others. Of course the most revered model is the annual Christmas celebration at the original Bethlehem in Palestine, where Jesus was born.

Christmas music is a wonderful tradition dating back to the Angelic choir (heavenly host) who reputedly "sang" God's praises at the birth of Jesus in Bethlehem (Lk 2:13) — though the verse doesn't actually say so. Yet no Christmas worship service or pageant is complete without Christmas music — whether it be Christmas carols or the magnificent classical music of Handel's "Messiah."

"Silent Night," a favorite carol, had an unusual beginning. In the Austrian village of Obendorf a Christmas crisis had occurred. When preparing for the Christmas mass the church organist, Franz Gruber, was shocked to find that the organ had broken down. "What can we do?" he asked the church's young priest, Joseph Mohr.

The young priest suggested Gruber set Mohr's new Christmas poem to music so the congregation could then sing it to the accompaniment of Gruber's guitar. Thus it was that night the joyful worshippers first heard the immortal words, "Silent night. Holy night. All is calm, all is bright ..."

Handel's world-famous cantata, the "Messiah," traditionally sung at Christmas had its own unique beginning. Struggling to make a living in London with his music, composer George Frederick Handel went hungry some days. One night in 1741 he wandered the streets lonely and depressed. Returning home he found a thick envelope containing Biblical references to the Messiah, Jesus Christ, which had been left at his door by the man who wrote lyrics for him, Charles Jennens.

Inspired by the Biblical words, "Comfort ye, comfort ye my people, saith your God ... The people who walked in darkness have seen a great light ... For unto you a child is born ... Glory to God in the highest ... Hallelujah, hallelujah," Handel joyfully began composing Christmas music. For three weeks he wrote at a feverish pace, hardly taking time to eat or sleep. So caught up in the words and music was he that Handel felt like he had been transported to heaven. With tears streaming down his face he admitted, "I do believe I have seen all of heaven before me, and the great God himself."

Hearing his wonderful creation, others have also enjoyed a touch of heaven. The first to hear this glorious Christmas music was an audience in Dublin, Ireland in 1742. They gave the piece a greater ovation than had ever been given to a concert in the city's history. Some weeks later an audience in London had a similar joyful experience. During the "Hallelujah Chorus" the king was so moved he rose to his feet. Thus started a custom still observed today. The "Messiah" won worldwide acclaim for Handel, and is still enjoyed by millions throughout the world.

Secular Christmas music has also won an honored place in many lands. Hearing Bing Crosby sing "White Christmas" is possible all over the world, just as children everywhere seem to claim "Rudolph, the Red-nosed Reindeer," not to mention

"Frosty, the Snowman." And what Christmas can be celebrated without singing "Jingle Bells" at least once, with "Deck the Halls with Boughs of Holly" or "Santa Claus is Coming to Town" as encores.

"I'll be Home for Christmas" brings tears to the eyes of those unable to return home for a traditional family Christmas celebration. They dream of lavish turkey dinners with dressing and red cranberry sauce, plus mountains of snow-white mashed potatoes, colorful vegetable plates with neatly cut green celery sticks side by side with yellow carrots. The crowning event of the family Christmas dinner is a choice of pumpkin, apple or mincemeat pie. Prior to the meal, or following it, are delicious drinks of eggnog or hot cider, along with rich fruitcake. All of this is accompanied with joyful greetings of "Merry Christmas!" and the loving exchange of Christmas gifts, usually wrapped in red or green paper, with gift boxes tied up with brightly colored ribbon and decorated with a fancy bow.

Christmas caroling customs vary from country to country. Carolers try to sound like the original Angel choir that led the shepherds to Bethlehem to attend Jesus' birth. Often they sing to neighbors and friends, but many such groups make it a point of spreading holiday cheer in nursing homes or other such isolating places. Thankfully, the custom of preparing Christmas dinners and parties for the needy and homeless is a custom that is growing.

The central event for celebrating Christmas is a worship service, followed by pageants, home meetings, caroling and programs for the needy. On the mission field Christmas is a glorious opportunity to tell the story of Jesus as Savior to people who are curious about this growing custom.

The first year I was in Japan I was involved in more than

15 Christmas services and programs in churches, schools, homes and even in factories (for hundreds of workers). In churches the emphasis was on worship and pageants, in schools it was a pageant. In homes it was informal worship and fellowship which prevailed while in factories it was telling the Christmas Story and singing Christmas carols and songs.

Throughout the years I served the church in Japan, we continued this practice annually for at Christmas the Japanese seemed more open and receptive to the good news of God's love, forgiveness and eternal life, provided through the Christ of Christmas. Though the origins of the Christmas holiday are hazy, the reality of Christ's coming to earth is reason enough to praise God — as did the angels in Bethlehem — and to commemorate this event annually, wishing peace and goodwill towards all people on earth.

2

Santa Claus, Christmas Trees and Advent Wreath Traditions

In a Christian school in Japan a teacher wanted to know how much her new Japanese students knew about Christmas. "Who was born at Christmas time?" she asked. She knew they ate "Christmas Decoration Cake" but did they know why?

"I know teacher, I know," replied an eager young lad, "It was Santa Claus!"

Since Santa Claus was the emphasis in department-store decorations and "Rudolph the Red-nosed Reindeer" and "Santa Claus is Coming to Town" were songs heard at Christmas on Japanese airwaves, it was no wonder.

Sadly, all over the world many people emphasize Santa Claus at Christmas time more than they do the Christ child born at Bethlehem. Although Santa Claus is seen as a secular tradition its beginning is attributed to a Christian saint, Saint

Nicholas, who was a native of the city of Patara in Lycia, Asia Minor (now Turkey).

As a youth Nicholas, a devoted Christian, entered the monastery at Sion, near Myra. Eventually he became bishop of the metropolitan church of Myra. Tradition says he was persecuted by the Roman Emperor Diocletian, then tortured and kept in prison until the reign of the more benevolent Emperor Constantine. Later St. Nicholas became the patron saint of Greece and Old Russia. In Holland he was seen as the patron saint of sailors and children.

Tradition says St. Nicholas gave gifts and money to the poor. One legend credits him with helping three daughters of a poor family by throwing a bag of money for each one's marriage dowry through a window at night. He would secretly deliver his gifts at night so no one would know who left them.

In Dutch St. Nicholas was called "Sinter Klass" and was usually depicted dressed as a bishop with miter and crosier riding a white horse. The custom has grown in Holland for children to leave wooden shoes (sometimes stockings) outside their doors on the eve of December sixth and fill them with hay to feed Sinter Klass' horse. Sinter comes that night and replaces the hay with cookies and candies. The Dutch brought this tradition to America in the 1600s where in English "Sinter Klass" became "Santa Claus." The shoes or stockings the Dutch left outside became stockings moved inside, hung by the fireplace.

In 1822 Clement C. Moore completely redesigned the image of Santa Claus, giving him a fur-trimmed red suit, a plump jolly figure, riding in a sleigh drawn by reindeer. It was Clement Moore who had Santa coming down the chimney to deliver his bag of gifts — which he described in a poem he wrote for his children entitled, "A Visit from St. Nicholas". The cartoonist

Thomas Nast solidified this new image of Santa Claus with sketches published in *Harper's Weekly* during the Civil War.

In America the annual lighting of a magnificent Christmas tree on the lawn of the President's "White House" is a joyful event — watched by millions on TV. But it is to Germany that we owe the origin of the Christmas tree tradition. Tradition says that in the 1600s Black Forest tribes in Germany brought evergreens inside to celebrate the winter solstice. Evergreens were seen as symbolizing long life, because they stay green even in cold winters. The Scandinavian people adopted this custom, for they too admired their many evergreen trees. In 1841, Albert, consort of Queen Victoria, introduced the Christmas tree custom to Great Britain and from there it migrated to the U.S. Some claim Hessian mercenary soldiers brought the custom to America during the Revolutionary War and German settlers in Pennsylvania reputedly had Christmas trees by 1746.

Today Christmas trees are often decorated with a combination of colored glass balls, electric lights of various colors, tinsel and small figures. These may represent the Holy Family, angels, shepherds, Magi and often Santa Claus, or they are in the shape of candles and bells. More humble decorations are often popular such as popcorn or cranberries strung on long threads or homemade figures and objects made of salvaged tinfoil. Also cotton may be used for "snow".

The "Chrismon Tree" is a new tradition developing among churches that want to decorate trees with symbols that refer more directly to Jesus Christ. The word "Chrismon" is a combination of Chris(t) and Mon(ogram), therefore the effort is to use monograms of Christ. This new tradition began in the Lutheran Church of the Ascension in Danville, Virginia, in 1957. In subsequent years ornaments were made of monograms as well as signs or symbols which refer to Jesus Christ. The practice is to have all Chrismons done in white or gold — white being the liturgical color for Christmas signifying Christ's purity and perfection and gold referring to Christ's majesty and glory. The lights represent Christ as the light of the world.

Many churches light Advent candles. The Advent wreath is usually made of evergreens with a place for four colored candles around a white "Christ Candle" in the center. There are many variations of the symbolism of the candles but it is common to have three violet candles and one pink candle around the white Christ candle — the vital center. During Advent one more candle is lit each subsequent Sunday until all are lit, with the Christ candle finally being lit Christmas Day.

The first violet candle has been called the Prophecy Candle, announcing the period of waiting. The second violet candle is symbolic of the preparation being made to receive the Christ child and is called the Bethlehem Candle. The third to be lit, the pink candle, typifies the act of sharing Christ and is the Shepherds' Candle. The fourth candle is the Angels' Candle, and is the candle of love and of the final coming. This is again violet. All of the candles symbolize Christ bringing light into our dark world.

[The *Chrismons: Basic Series* is available from The Ascension Lutheran Church, 314 W. Main St., Danville, VA 24541.]

3

Christmas Cards, Mistletoe, Holly, the Wassail Bowl, Yule Log and Two Stories

The ubiquitous Christmas card tradition began in England. In 1843 Sir Henry Cole, a British businessman, printed a thousand lithographed, hand-colored cards designed by the artist John Horsly and sold them for a shilling each. Enterprising business people in other countries soon followed Sir Henry's example, creating a popular and lucrative new industry.

Kissing under the mistletoe at Christmas time has become popular in many countries. Though the origins of this tradition are hazy, in the fifth century the scholar Pliny reported that white-robed Druids clipped mistletoe from oak trees to be used as charms against evil. In Scandinavia it is said that when enemies happened to meet under a tree with mistletoe they were obliged to lay down their weapons, embrace like friends, and keep peace together the remainder of the day. This may be how the custom of kissing under the mistletoe migrated to England and from there to America.

A German legend says Christ's crown of thorns was made from holly. Romans thought holly had power as a medicine and some even believed it contained magical powers. Some ancient people felt holly's lustrous green leaves and bright red berries were symbols of eternal life and since holly bore fruit in winter, it was considered one of the most favored plants in nature. As Christianity spread from country to country holly became a symbol of eternal life. Today, holly is used in Christmas wreaths along with mistletoe and other evergreens.

The Christmas wassail bowl comes from an ancient Saxon drinking custom among a Germanic people who settled in Britain in the fifth century. The Saxons chose the wassail bowl with great care as to its size and beauty and placed arcs of evergreens over the top of the bowl as a decoration. The drink was a mixture of hot ale, sugar, nutmeg or ginger, decorated with baked apples. In England Christmas carolers often took along a wassail bowl so going "wassailing" meant going to a friend's home to sing carols and then offer the friends a drink from the wassail bowl. Carolers often *receive* refreshments.

In Germany the Teutonic Yule Feast provided the tradition of a yule log for the Christmas celebration. The yule log was the foundation log for the fireplace, and the fire symbolized warmth and light in the cold dark winter. In some places the foundation yule log was so important that a part of it was retained to light the new yule log of the following year. For Christmas, the yule log symbolizes the warmth and light Christ has given to the people of the world.

One of the most famous stories about Christmas is *A Christmas Carol* by the British writer Charles Dickens. Published in 1843, this short story has gained popularity far and wide. Its most infamous character has become part of our common parlance so that now "Scrooge" symbolizes any mean-spirited curmudgeon who refuses to celebrate Christmas.

In brief, the story begins Christmas Eve with Ebenezer Scrooge, a selfish, disagreeable merchant in London, returning to his living quarters with no thought of celebrating the holiday. He has spurned an invitation to spend Christmas with his nephew Fred and only reluctantly gave a one-day holiday to his overworked, underpaid clerk, Bob Cratchit. Asked to give to charity in the name of his dead partner, Jacob Marley, he retorts that the Christmas spirit is foolish and wasteful. After Scrooge goes to sleep that night he sees three apparitions — the Ghosts of Christmas past, Christmas present and Christmas yet to come. This experience brings about a complete change in Scrooge who becomes instead a generous, kind and thoughtful man. He takes a basket of food to Bob Cratchit's home on Christmas Day and continues to be kindly toward others throughout the coming years.

People all over the world repeat the beloved words spoken by Bob Cratchit and his crippled son, Tiny Tim. When Bob makes the toast, "A Merry Christmas to us all, my dears. God bless us," Tiny Tim replies, "God bless us every one."

Another Christmas story which is not as well known but equally poignant is *The Story of the Other Wise Man* by Henry van Dyke. The author admits the story came to him one night as "a gift" when he was "full of sickness and sorrow ... tormented with pain." First published in 1895 as a small booklet, it has been translated into many languages and is in thousands of libraries all over the world.

The story tells of Artaban, a Magi who studied the stars and read prophecy. He knew that the messiah was going to be born and made preparations to go and see the Baby Jesus along with the Three Magi. Artaban had three wonderful gifts to give to Jesus — an emerald, a ruby and a beautiful pearl.

On his way to meet the Three Magi, Artaban stopped to care for a dying man. Due to this delay, he missed his three friends and they went on without him. Artaban then had to sell his emerald to get the supplies needed to travel across the desert. He arrived in Bethlehem too late to see Jesus (Mary and Joseph having fled by then into Egypt) but in time to save a woman's baby from Herod's murderous soldiers. He bought the baby's life with the second of his gifts for Jesus, the ruby. Continuing on his search for the one who would be king of all, Artaban was told by an old rabbi that the king he sought would not be found in a palace, nor among the rich and powerful, but among the poor, the lowly, the oppressed.

Many years passed for Artaban. During his life of searching, he cared for people, fed the hungry, clothed the naked, healed the sick and brought comfort to the prisoner. But he had not forgotten his quest and 33 years later he still sought the Christ-child. Worn and weary and ready to die, but still looking for the king, Artaban came for the last time to Jerusalem.

It was Passover and many people seem agitated. Asking what was happening, he was told there was to be a crucifixion and one to be crucified was the man called Jesus of Nazareth who had spoken of a new kingdom — the kingdom of God. Artaban's heart filled with hope. If this were the king he had looked for then he would try to save him by buying his life from the cross with his pearl.

But Artaban was stopped by a young woman who was being sold into slavery. She begged him to help her. He did the only thing he considered possible and gave the last gift he had saved for the Christ-child, a magnificent pearl, to the young woman. Although he had helped the young woman, Artaban felt terrible grief. Nothing would stop the crucifixion now.

Darkness filled the air and the ground shook. The house that Artaban was in fell to the ground. When the dust cleared, Artaban lay dying without hope of ever knowing his King. But the voice of Christ said to him: "Truly I say unto you, inasmuch as you have done it unto one of the least of these my brethren, you have done it unto me." Artaban's whole life had been one of service to his Lord and God. His journey was ended, his treasures accepted. The fourth Magi had found the King and his name was Jesus.

These two classic Christmas stories have been told and re-told over the years, but no one ever seems to tire to hear about and celebrate the birth of our Lord and Savior Jesus Christ. Might we all be like Artaban living lives of service to the Christ of Christmas.

4

Brief Biographical Sketches
of the Contributors

Florence Antablin — Twice Florence and her husband Bill have been forced out of the mission fields where they worked. After 13 years as missionaries in Syria and Lebanon, war drove them out of the country. Then after four years serving as chaplains to expatriate people living and working in Saudi Arabia, they were expelled by fanatic Muslim clergy and the secret police who claimed that as "keepers of the Muslim holy sites of Mecca and Medina," they could not allow the Antablins to conduct Christian services in Saudi Arabia even if they were only for foreign Christians. The Antablins continued their ministry in interim pastorates both in the U.S. and Egypt. They have retired to California.

Thelma Appleton — While serving at Silliman University in the Philippines, Thelma was appointed dean of women at the university where her husband also taught. In addition she taught Christian education in the divinity school and worked with children and women for the Filipino churches. She is now retired in Pasadena, California.

Rev. Dr. Marcia Mary Ball — For 32 years Marcia served as a missionary teacher and ordained minister for the United Methodist Church, most of that time in Zimbabwe, Africa. "My life and ministry have been a joyous experience!" she says from her active "retirement" in Claremont, California.

Rev. Gayle Beanland — Born in Cameroon, Africa, Gayle returned there as a missionary following in his parents footsteps. Having gained special audiovisual skills while serving in the U.S. military, Gayle used this ability to help the African people, in addition to providing pastoral care and evangelism services. As director of an audiovisual center in Cameroon he ministered as a communication consultant throughout Africa. In retirement Gayle uses his skills to direct a closed-circuit TV program whose goal is to help shut-ins and nursing-home residents in his retirement community in Duarte, California.

Mildred R. Brown — Because her parents were missionaries in China, Mildred was born in that country. However her father's health problems forced her family to come home while she was still a toddler. Burdened to continue the missionary task begun by her parents, Millie early began planning to become a missionary. Following this missionary call, Millie taught in Japan's snowy city of Sapporo for over 35 years, teaching English and Bible. In retirement Millie continued to teach English as a second language to those who needed it in California. Her health began to fail, so she had to give this up in 1995. Millie died in July, 1996.

Rev. Robert Caldwell — The Christmas-tree fire that singed off Bob's eyelashes and arm hair happened while he was a seminary student pastor in Moundsville, West Virginia. In over 40 years of ministry, Bob served churches in West Virginia, Iowa and California. After retiring in 1975 Bob continued to hold four interim pastorates in California and two in New Zealand. He continues an active preaching schedule from his home in Duarte, California.

Rev. Dr. Kenn and Mrs. Sue Carmichael — Kenn and Sue worked as communication consultants, especially for the Radio Voice of the Gospel in Ethiopia. For 20 years they ministered to the church in the Middle East, East Africa, Jerusalem and the U.S. Kenn was also a writer-director of many church films including the "Mark of the Hawk" and "Seventy Times Seven." Before taking up a very active retirement in California they served a church in Lafayette, Indiana. Kenn passed away in March, 1996.

Kirby Filson Davis writes about Christmas in the beautiful but often snowy state of Colorado where she lived and ministered with her husband, Hal, who pastored four churches over a period of 30 years. Kirby grew up in Chicago where her father was a professor at McCormick Seminary. Now retired in California in the same retirement community as her mother, 98, Kirby edits the newsletter for the community.

Rev. James B. Douthitt — Jim began his ministry in Iowa, Colorado and Nebraska before accepting a call to serve the Navajo church. Jim says, "My most memorable Christmas was my first one as pastor at Ganado Mission in Arizona. At 'Camp Christmas,' 2000 Navajos came for a grand celebration." After ministering to the Navajo church for nine years, he accepted a call to Whittier, California where he stayed 20 years. He has two books of poetry published. Now retired, Jim, 86, plays tennis regularly.

Rev. Dr. J. Lawrence Driskill — Larry's greatest challenge as a missionary to Japan was organizing the first church in Japan's *Senri Newtown* — a "newtown" for 150,000 people built quickly by the government as a bedroom community for workers in Japan's second largest city, Osaka. With the able assistance of his wife Lillian plus Japanese coworkers, Larry organized three new churches in Japan and helped developed six others. Larry has five published books on mission topics. Retired at Westminster Gardens in Duarte, California, at 75 he enjoys being the youngster, playing tennis with his elders, Jim Douthitt, 86, and Frank Newman, 90.

Florence Galloway — After training in nursing and theology, Florence and her husband Ralph served for many years as missionaries in Africa, first in Cameroon and then in Zaire. Seeing the great health needs of African families, Florence specialized in promoting wellness concerns and family health. Her good work helped save the lives of countless people in Africa. Now retired, Florence and Ralph continue to minister to their retirement community and nearby churches.

Rev. Ralph Galloway — Born in Egypt where his parents were missionaries, Ralph spent his first 14 years there. After serving in the U.S. Naval Reserve in World War II, Ralph completed seminary training and then went to Africa as a missionary along with his wife Florence. Although they were involved in some evangelistic work, their main concerns centered on promoting health matters in Africa and in school administration, first in Cameroon and then in Zaire. He retired to Pasadena, California and continues to care for his community with the same Christian spirit which he showed in Africa.

Rev. Joseph Gray — After seminary and three pastorates in the Midwest, Joe was appointed missionary to the Navajos on their reservation at Chinle, Arizona. Here he worked for 19 years. Perhaps the finest tribute to Joe from the Navajos he served was their request that his wife, Mildred, be the first white person buried at their reservation church, showing their love for Joe and Mildred. At 90 and retired, Joe still helps others.

Rev. Dr. Harold Hanlin — Harold was a U.S. Navy Chaplain stationed in the Marshall Islands during World War II. After finishing seminary, Harold earned a Ph.D. from Southern Baptist Seminary in Louisville, KY. Ordained by the Christian Church (Disciples of Christ), he taught New Testament Greek at Butler University and served three pastorates before becoming a Navy chaplain in 1945. Approaching his 90th birthday, Harold today is grateful that his life partner in ministry, Mary Ruth, is still by his side. They have retired to Claremont, California and are surrounded by loving and helpful friends there.

Nannie Hereford — Nannie was born in Osaka, Japan where her parents served as missionaries. Following her parents' example, Nannie became a missionary to Japan, teaching in Japan's cold, snowy city of Sapporo. Forced out by approaching war, Nannie became a teacher in the Philippines where she was caught by the invading Japanese army, interned and almost starved from malnutrition before being rescued by American soldiers. On release Nannie returned to Japan where she worked as an evangelistic missionary for many years. On retiring Nannie continues to be active in church and community service in Nashville, Tennessee.

Elizabeth A. Hessel — Betty's special interest during the 23 years of missionary service in the Philippines was leprosy work. When she married Eugene Hessel in 1932 both were interested in mission work. Their departure was delayed 14 years by the Depression during which time they served churches in the U.S. In the Philippines they both worked on the staff of Union Theological Seminary until illness forced them to return to the U.S. in 1969. They have returned often to the Philippines for volunteer service. Now retired in California, they keep very active.

Rev. Nicholas M. Iyoya — Nick was born in Japan and came to the U.S. at age ten. Disillusioned by the Holocaust and the bombing of Hiroshima, Nick lost faith in humanistic and idealistic answers to human progress, but through reading the Bible he became a Christian. Nick has served three Japanese-American churches in California and one in New York. Together with his wife Rhoda he served two years as a missionary fraternal worker. Retired in Pasadena, California, they continue to do volunteer work in nearby churches.

Rev. Dr. Robert Lazear — After working with his father on a ranch in Wyoming, Bob left his cowboy life to serve as a missionary in Colombia and Spain. During 40 years of ministry, Bob has found time to write four books in Spanish. His colleagues in Colombia say, "Bob was one of our best missionaries and a joy to work with." In his retirement community Bob continues to translate Spanish hymns for others to enjoy singing.

Eleanor van Lierop — Eleanor's exacting, yet rewarding, missionary work in Korea was in rescuing former prostitutes and unwed mothers from a hopeless condition. With training as a social worker, Eleanor helped to organize and direct the Aeron Institute which has rehabilitated many women in Korea. She also taught English at Yonsei University in Seoul where her husband Peter was a professor. After 30 years service in Korea they have retired to California but keep involved in ministry to surrounding churches.

Clara Lindholm — In 1931 Clara went to China as a bride with her husband Paul to begin mission work. She taught until they were forced out of China by war. They then went to the Philippines but again had to flee, now with four children, to the mountains to escape capture by the invading Japanese. Helped by Filipino Christians they survived two years in hiding. In 1944 she and the children were evacuated to Australia via submarine and then to the U.S. by hospital ship. Reunited with Paul in 1945, she continued mission work until retiring.

Rev. Dr. Bob & Mrs. Esther McIntire — Bob and Esther helped organize the Centro Audio Visual Evangelico (CAVE) in Brazil to serve Latin America. Bob also taught at the seminary in Campinas. After 30 years of missionary service, Bob and Esther ministered to retirees in Mid-America before retiring themselves to Westminster Gardens in California. There Bob took the lead in organizing closed-circuit TV programs for physically challenged retirees. They continue to volunteer for this helpful ministry.

Betty Newman — Leaving her native Canada to do nurses' training in the U.S., Betty met a young intern who swept her away — to China, that is, where they served together as medical missionaries for 15 years. Tried as foreign spies by the Communists, they were kicked out of China whereupon they went to Cameroon, Africa where they worked for 13 years. One of Betty's "miracles" is that after being unconscious on a tennis court with no heartbeat for eight minutes, she was "brought back to life" by CPR from her husband and medics. Betty still walks daily.

Dr. Frank Newman — Frank's medical missionary service in China ended abruptly in 1948 after he and his family were tried and expelled as "foreign spies" by the new Communist regime. They avoided prison and execution because their Chinese Christian friends pretended to turn against them shouting, "kick the foreign devils out of our country." After this stint in China, Frank and his wife Betty continued to serve as medical missionaries in the very different setting of Cameroon, Africa, until they retired.

Dorothy Parker — For 32 years Dorothy worked in India heading up a church literature program. During this time, with the help of various Indian pastors, writers and teachers, she published many handbooks, pamphlets and study guides. These not only have been widely used in the churches throughout the continent for study and growth, but they have proved to be effective and helpful evangelistic tools by Christians wanting to spread the gospel to their Hindu and Muslim neighbors. Dorothy is currently retired and living in California.

Rev. Fred Schneider — Fred's main objective as a missionary to Argentina and Brazil was to train pastors in those countries. This proved especially difficult during the time of the Peronist dictatorship in Argentina, and Fred had many unhappy dealings with the federal police investigating their Christian work for signs of subversion. As president of the seminary, Fred had to endure this harassment and oppression. Thankfully churches in both countries are now thriving. Fred and his wife Alma have retired to Claremont, California.

Rev. Dr. Richard Smith — Dick's work with miners in Scotts Run, West Virginia, received national attention in *Life* and *Time* magazines as well as a cover story in *Presbyterian Life*. In addition Dick was a professor at San Francisco Theological Seminary and with his wife Bea organized seven churches in Brazil, in Mexico and the U.S. After retiring in 1979 they served international churches in Bangkok, Thailand and Tokyo, Japan.

Beatrice Stevenson — Born in China, Beatrice (known as "Bunny" to her friends) returned to that country after finishing her training. Along with her husband Ted she worked as a medical missionary in China for five years until they were forced out by war. Later when Ted was interned in the Philippines by Japanese invaders, Bunny took care of their four boys all alone. After the war they remained in the States for awhile because of their sons' educational needs, but eventually when the boys were old enough, Bunny and Ted returned to their overseas work to help provide medical care for over a thousand missionaries on the field. Even after retirement Bunny and Ted went as volunteer medical missionaries to India and Kenya.

Marabelle Taylor — Marabelle holds a record for making an early career decision. When only 3½ she met a missionary to Africa and immediately decided to become a missionary nurse to Africa. For over 30 years Marabelle served as a missionary nurse in Africa, first in mission hospitals and then for 20 years she supervised the care of motherless babies in her own home, hiring young African girls to help her. With their fine assistance, she was able to provide medical care also for people in the remote Babimbi Hill of Cameroon using her mobile clinic. Even in retirement, Marabelle, now 80, continues to help nursing home residents in her California community.

Rev. Dr. Harold Wilke — Born without hands, Dr. Wilke became an international expert in various aspects of rehabilitation medicine, combining both medical and spiritual remedies. He has lectured and consulted in 55 countries on this subject — and was invited to the White House to participate in the presidential signing of the "Americans With Disabilities Act" offering a blessing for this occasion. When President Bush gave him his signature pen Harold accepted it with his toes, since he has no hands. Harold often travels alone taking care of all his own needs. He is an ordained minister in the United Church of Christ, which he has served for over 50 years as a pastor, church executive and seminary professor.

Rev. Dr. J. Christy Wilson, Jr. — After being involved in a "tent-making" ministry as an English teacher in Kabul, Afghanistan, Christy became pastor of a church there for expatriate Christians living and working in Kabul. When an unfriendly prime minister came to power he ordered the church destroyed. After leveling the church to the ground the workmen dug six feet further down because they had heard rumors about an "underground church." Forced out of Afghanistan, Christy taught at Gordon-Conwell Seminary and was interim director of Zwemer Institute, a ministry to Muslims, before retiring in California.

Additional copies of this book may be obtained
from your local bookstore,
or by sending $13.45 per paperback copy, postpaid,
or $22.45 per library hardcover copy, postpaid,
to:

Hope Publishing House
P.O. Box 60008
Pasadena, CA 91116

CA residents please add 8¼% sales tax
FAX orders to: (818) 792-2121
Telephone VISA/MC orders to (800) 326-2671